PRINCIPALITIES AND POWERS
IN THE
NEW TESTAMENT

ABOUT THE BOOK

Under the title "Principalities and Powers" and a number
of other synonyms, the New Testament is studded with
texts referring to the domination of the world, its institutions, and its "atmosphere" by Satan. These texts are analys-
ed in order to present an overall picture of this spirit of
Evil, which by temptation and deception attempts to lead
men into sin. Christ's coming is shown as the definitive
defeat of the Powers which, with only a future of damnation before them, must make a last effort to inveigle the
Christian by disbelief and disobedience away from the
victorious Christ. This study is a valuable contribution to
a subject which has produced little literature. The author
is professor of Ancient Christian Literature and New Testament Exegesis in the University of Bonn.

QUAESTIONES DISPUTATAE

HEINRICH SCHLIER

PRINCIPALITIES AND POWERS
IN THE
NEW TESTAMENT

HERDER AND HERDER

225.7 × 6
scP .07
.07?

1st Edition 1961
2nd Impression 1961
3rd Impression 1962

HERDER AND HERDER NEW YORK

232 Madison Avenue, New York 16, N.Y.

Original edition "Mächte und Gewalten im Neuen Testament", Herder, Freiburg.

225.7

Library of Congress Catalog Card Number: 61-9373
First published in West Germany © 1961 Herder KG
Made and printed in West Germany by Herder

CONTENTS

Introduction   7

  I Nature and operations of the principalities . .   11

 II Jesus Christ and the principalities   40

III The Christian and the principalities   53

Antichrist   69

INTRODUCTION

IT is only when we read the New Testament attentively that we note the frequent references to "principalities and powers", as St. Paul calls those forces which are mentioned in almost all parts of the New Testament. They appear under various names in the oldest sources of the Synoptic Gospels; in 1 Thessalonians, as well as in the Epistles to the Colossians and Ephesians: the Gospel of St. John mentions them, as does the second Epistle of St. Peter, which is also a late work.

But they are mentioned often in these writings within the framework of traditions which had already been formulated and handed down as official statements of the faith of the early Christian community. We find their names in passages which either cite or allude to sermon paradigms, formalized kerygma, primitive professions of faith, and hymns and eucharistic prayers.[1] We have only to think of the brief summary of the γενόμενον ῥῆμα, of redemption, in Acts 10:37 et seq., or of the primitive profession of faith in the hymn to Christ in Phil. 2:5 et seq. Other examples are the passage about wisdom in 1 Cor. 2:7 et seq., the prayer of thanksgiving in Col. 1:12 et seq., and the Baptism hymn in 1 Peter 3:18 et seq. This last passage, for example, calls out in triumph: "Who is on the right hand of

---

[1] Cf. O. Cullmann, *Christus und die Zeit* (1946), pp. 132–5; 133, note 13; 170; *idem, Die ersten christlichen Glaubensbekenntnisse* (2nd ed., 1949), pp. 53 et seq.; *idem, Der Staat im Neuen Testament* (1956), p. 72.

God . . . being gone into heaven, the angels and powers and virtues being made subject to him."

These texts show beyond doubt that, from the earliest age, the Church's preaching and professions of faith contained references to what we call "principalities and powers". And this fact is confirmed if we look beyond the New Testament to the Apostolic Fathers, who are the first echoes of the Apostles' preaching, or to the New Testament apocrypha, which were early popular writings. It is also evident in the work of the first Apologists.[2]

Any survey of early Christian literature shows that belief in these principalities was firmly established in the apostolic faith of the primitive Church. It is, therefore, a matter of importance for readers of the New Testament, and particularly for theologians, to determine what exactly these powers are. Biblical exegesis is, of course, the first method to adopt in the search for an answer.[3] Indeed, some bible scholars have done something to prepare the ground.[4] Their studies approach the

[2] For example, Ignatius, Eph. 13:2; 17:1; Trall. 9:1; Polycarp, Phil. 2:1; Justin, Ap. 1, 42:4; Dial. 41:1; 85:1, et seq.; Tatian, Or. 29; especially the apocryphal "Acts" of the apostles. See H. Schlier, *Christus und die Kirche im Epheserbrief* (1930), pp. 6 et seq.

[3] As far as I can see, Catholic theologians in modern times have devoted little attention to the "principalities", perhaps because the biblical scholars themselves have not raised the problem. However, J. Binktrine, for example, has devoted about twenty pages to the principalities (the fallen angels), in his book *Die Lehre von der Schöpfung* (1956) – a work which deals at length (pp. 87–203) with angels.

[4] Cf. O. Everling, *Die paulinische Angelologie und Dämonologie* (1888); M. Dibelius, *Die Geisterwelt im Glauben des Paulus* (1909); G. Kurze, *Der Engels- und Teufelsglaube des Apostels Paulus* (1915); K. L. Schmidt, "Die Natur- und Geisteskräfte im paulinischen Erkennen und Glauben"

question from the angle of Comparative Religion – an obvious approach to the matter. They have attempted to elucidate the linguistic basis as well as the ideas and experiences behind the New Testament statements. They assembled the material of pre-Christian terms and notions with which the New Testament concepts are connected; they traced their history, explained relationships and clarified analogies in order to determine the point of origin of the New Testament expressions. This kind of work is very necessary, but it is indeed not sufficient to solve the problem, which phenomena are meant by these powers. It is quite legitimate, as well as useful, to trace ideas and names – as far as this process is applicable – to Jewish or Hellenistic sources, or again beyond these to Babylon or Iran, and to show in detail what it was that the New Testament inherited. But in order to know what is meant by these principalities, that kind of investigation is of little avail. Biblical scholarship, however, ought to be ultimately concerned with that meaning. Its object is to identify the reality which is expressed in the language and ideas of the New Testament. Or can it be that no reality at all corresponds to the terms "principalities and powers"? While the New Testament attaches importance to them, it is occasionally suggested that they are merely fictions of the imagery of ancient mythology, perhaps only allegories of a quite different reality, which, so it is said, have unfortunately been retained by the New Testament, although such myths

in *Eranos-Jahrbuch,* 14 (1947), pp. 87–143; B. Noack, *Satanas und Soteria. Untersuchungen zur neutestamentlichen Daemonologie* (1948). See also Strack-Billerbeck, IV, pp. 501–35: "Zur altjüdischen Daemonologie"; H. Bietenhard, *Die himmlische Welt im Urchristentum und Spätjudentum* (1951). See also the relevant articles in *Theologisches Wörterbuch* (ThWB).

and allegories ought to have been discarded from the Christian Faith long ago.

The New Testament texts, at any rate, challenge scholars to investigate these phenomena, emphasized as they are by their authors as having an important place within Christ's redemptive act.

It must be clearly stated in advance that only exegesis can attempt to solve the problem, for to us nowadays these phenomena seem strange, and the concepts which the New Testament employs to understand them largely meaningless.

In the present state of our theological and biblical studies it is even more important to ask the right question than to provide an answer. To do so we shall bypass many details and concentrate upon a general idea of our subject.

For this purpose the New Testament itself provides us with three main perspectives. The nature and operations of these principalities are outlined in various texts. We then come to their "history" under the influence of Jesus Christ. Finally we shall examine the attitude which Christians ought to adopt towards them.

I

NATURE AND OPERATIONS OF THE PRINCIPALITIES

THE principalities and powers are variously described in the New Testament, and their names repay examination, for they shed some light on their nature.

They are referred to, both in the singular and in the plural, as principalities (ἀρχαί), powers (ἐξουσίαι), and virtues (δυνάμεις).[5] We read also of dominions (κυριότητες), thrones (θρόνοι) and names (ὀνόματα).[6] Other titles are – both in the singular and the plural – princes (ἄρχοντες), the princes of this world (ἄρχοντες τοῦ κόσμου [αἰῶνος]), lords (κύριοι), gods (θεοί), angels (ἄγγελοι), devils (δαιμόνια, δαίμονες), spirits (πνεύματα), unclean or wicked spirits (πνεύματα ἀκάθαρτα, πονηρά), spirits of wickedness (πνευματικὰ τῆς πονηρίας), and elements (στοιχεῖα).[7] There is also mention of Satan (ὁ σατανᾶς) or the devil (ὁ διάβολος), who is called Beelzebub (βεελζεβούλ) and Belial (βελίαρ), and is

[5] Rom. 8:38; 1 Cor. 15:24; Eph. 1:21; 3:10; 6:12; Col. 1:16; 2:10, 15. [6] Eph. 1:21; Col. 1:16; cf., 2 Peter 2:10; Jude 8.

[7] Mark 3:22 par (par. = synoptic parallel passages); John 12:31; 16:11; 14:30; 1 Cor. 2:6, 8; Eph. 2:2; 1 Cor. 8:5; 2 Cor. 4:4; Gal. 4:8; Rom. 8:38; 1 Cor. 4:9; 6:3; Col. 2:18; Matt. 25:41; 2 Cor. 12:7; 2 Peter 2:4; Jude 6; Apoc. 9:11; 12:7, 9; Matt. 7:22; 9:33, etc.; John 7:20, etc.; 1 Cor. 10:20 et seq.; 1 Tim. 4:1; Jas. 2:19; Apoc. 9:20; 16:14; 18:2; Matt. 8:31; 8:16; 10:1, etc.; Mark 1:23, 27, etc.; Acts 5:16; 8:7, etc.; 1 Cor. 2:12; Eph. 2:2; 1 John 4:1; 3, 6; Apoc. 16:13; 18:2; Eph. 6:12; Gal. 4:3, 9; Col. 2:8, 20.

designated by the mythical ideograms of the serpent (ὁ ὄφις), the dragon (ὁ δράκων), or the lion (ὁ λέων), as well as being named as the strong (ὁ ἰσχυρός), the wicked one (ὁ πονηρός), the accuser (ὁ κατήγωρ), the tempter (ὁ πειράζων), the destroyer (ὁ ὀλεθρευτής), the adversary (ὁ ἀντίδικος), and the enemy (ὁ ἐχθρός).[8] He also appears, as we have already seen, as the prince of devils (ὁ ἄρχων τῶν δαιμονίων), the prince of the world – or of this world (ὁ ἄρχων τοῦ κόσμου [τοῦ αἰῶνος τούτου]), the god of this world (ὁ θεὸς τοῦ αἰῶνος τούτου), and the prince of the power of this air (ὁ ἄρχων τῆς ἐξουσίας τοῦ ἀέρος).[9]

There is thus a large number of names for the principalities, and particularly for Satan, which in itself shows again how much Christians of the early Church were preoccupied with these phenomena.

Their names are derived only in few cases from the Old Testament, which indeed describes Satan as accuser and tempter,[10] but mentions him only three times. Demons were also known, but not as playing any part in the redemptive history of

[8] Matt. 4:10; 12:26, etc.; John 13:27; Acts 5:3; 26:18; Rom. 16:20; 1 Cor. 5:5, etc.; Apoc. 2:9, 13, etc.; Matt. 4:1, 5, 8, 11 etc.; John 6:70; 8:44; 13:2; Acts 10:38; 13:10; Eph. 4:27; 6:11; 1 Tim. 3:6, 7, 11; 2 Tim. 2:26; 3:3; Tit. 2:3; Heb. 2:14; Jas. 4:7; 1 Peter 5:8; 1 John 3:8, 10; Jude 9; Apoc. 2:10, etc.; Matt. 10:25; 12:24, 27, etc.; 2 Cor. 6:15; 2 Cor. 11:3; Apoc. 12:9, 14, 15; 20:2; Apoc. 12:3, 4, 7, etc.; 1 Peter 5:8; cf. 2 Tim. 4:17; Apoc. 13:2; Matt. 12:29 par.; Matt. 6:13; 13:19, 38; John 17:15; Eph. 6:16; 2 Thess. 3:3; 1 John 2:13, 14; 3:12; 5:18 (19); Apoc. 12:10; Matt. 4:3; 1 Thess. 3:5; 1 Cor. 10:10; 1 Peter 5:8 (2 Thess. 2:4); Matt. 13:25 et seq.; 1 Cor. 15:25 et seq., etc.; (Acts 13:10).

[9] Matt. 9:34; 12:24 par.; John 12:31; 14:30; 16:11; 1 Cor. 2:6, 8; Eph. 2, 2.

[10] ThWB, II, 71 et seq. (by Rad, Foerster).

12

Israel.[11] Hellenistic popular belief contributed little to these names. "Demon" which also appears occasionally in the Septuagint is, of course, a Greek word. The New Testament names for the principalities derive from Judaism, and particularly from Jewish apocalyptic writing. Judaism in turn had, of course, adopted some of them from neighbouring religions.[12]

We mention these facts because they give two indications about the nature of principalities. First, they obviously are phenomena such as had been seen and experienced outside Christendom, or, to be more precise, outside the revelation of the Old and New Testaments. In some way revelation absorbed them from the tradition of universal human experience. When they were mentioned by Jesus himself, or by the apostles and the early Church, their hearers, whether Jewish or Gentile, knew what was meant.

The second point only emerges from closer comparisons of New Testament statements with those of Jewish apocalyptic writings. Beside the variations in detail, the whole attitude of the New Testament towards these principalities differs from that of Judaism. The New Testament not only is much more reserved about them than many Jewish sources, or even Greek popular beliefs as expressed in the magic papyri, but it has also no theoretical or speculative interest in them. The New Testament nowhere gives an exact description of the various phenomena; there is no effort to differentiate among them, or to arrange the various names or appearances systematically. The New Testa-

---

[11] ThWB, II, 10 et seq. (Foerster).
[12] Cf. W. Bousset – H. Gressmann, *Die Religion des Judentums* (3rd ed., 1926), pp. 320 et seq.; pp. 331 et seq.; G. F. Moore, *Judaism in the First Centuries of the Christian Era* (7th ed., 1954), pp. 400 et seq.

ment has no counterpart to the treatise on angels, which we find in 1 Henoch 6–36; it also lacks a fully developed demonology. Basically, the New Testament is not concerned with a general philosophy of the world, since it regards this world either as a gift of God the Creator, or as an oppressive instrument of evil. In neither case is it open to man to do with it as he would in any human system. Similarly, the realm of principalities and demons is of interest to the New Testament only because they must be resisted and the world protected from them. So the nature of demons concerns the New Testament only as something which attacks men and must be resisted. It is only outside the New Testament, on the fringe of the early Church, in the Christian apocrypha and in Gnostic literature, that we find tendencies to seek for Gnosis of the demoniacal powers integrated into a total world view: this is illustrated by their aim, by no means confined to theory, to know "the depths of Satan" (Apoc. 2:24).

On the one hand, therefore, the New Testament quite openly adopted from Jewish and other merely human traditions the names for these principalities – and also, naturally, certain facts about them. On the other hand, it has obviously no interest in speculation or theory about them, as we shall see.

Examination shows that the names given to the powers of evil are, to a large extent, interchangeable. Naturally, certain New Testament writers favour one name rather than another: we all know that the Synoptic Gospels usually speak of Satan, the devil, demons or spirits; St. Paul often uses the names principalities, powers, or virtues,[13] while the Gospel of St. John prefers to speak of the prince of this world. But these names are

[13] In my opinion they are always wicked powers, that is, hostile to

not mutually exclusive; they are freely interchangeable. In St. Matthew's Gospel, as we have seen, Satan or the devil can also be called "the prince of devils",[14] while in St. John's Gospel Satan or the devil is the prince of this world;[15] St. Paul is speaking of him when he refers to "the god of this world", (2 Cor. 4:4) and to the "prince of the power of this air" (Eph. 2:2).

The same applies to the principalities and powers to which St. Paul often refers. He calls them powers, thrones, principalities,[16] and also angels,[17] in 2 Cor. 12:7, where he speaks of an "angel of Satan". St. Matthew speaks of the devil's angels (Matt. 25:41).[18] In some cases, as in Col. 2:8, Gal. 4:3–9, St. Paul calls them elements: in Gal. 4:8 these elements are called gods. Again the principalities and powers are "spirits of wickedness" (Eph. 6:12). These are identical with the spirits, wicked spirits, unclean spirits and demons of the Synoptic Gospels and Acts.[19] St. Paul links the demons with the gods and princes, and in some respects identifies them.

God and to Christ. This is true even of Eph. 1:21; 3:10; Col. 1:16; 2:10, for there is no reason for distinguishing the ἀρχαὶ καὶ ἐξουσίαι of these texts from those which are mentioned in Rom. 8:38; 1 Cor. 15:24; Eph. 6:12 and Col. 2:15; and in the latter texts they are certainly hostile powers. Nevertheless it can be said that they are creatures of God, and we shall explain afterwards (p. 37 et seq.), in what sense this is true. Sometimes, of course it is not the wickedness of their nature which is stressed, but some other quality, such as their power. And to that extent is it sometimes possible to have the impression that there are also "neutral" principalities, though, theologically, it is difficult to understand what they are supposed to be.   [14] Matt. 9:34; 12:26.
 [15] John 6:70; 8:44; 13:2; 13:27.   [16] Eph. 2:20; Col. 1:16; Rom. 8:38.
 [17] Rom. 8:38; Col. 2:18.   [18] Cf. 2 Cor. 11:14.
 [19] Cf. for example, Matt. 16:1 = Mark 3:14; Mark 6:7 = Luke 9:1; Mark 7:25, 26; Luke 10:17, 20.

The interchangeability of the various names for principalities is undisputable, yet what does it mean? To begin with, it indicates that the New Testament is not much concerned with individual names. Secondly, these names essentially refer to one and the same phenomenon. Finally, none of these traditional or conventional names allows us to understand this phenomenon. The concepts tell us something, but they do not convey the nature of the phenomenon.

Only one distinction is more accurately drawn, namely that demons, spirits, angels, principalities and powers are subordinate to Satan or the devil, as his innumerable powers. They are manifestations of his power.

In Mark 3:22 et seq., Beelzebub is called "the prince of devils". They carry out his instructions, and it is through them that he and his works come to us.[20] When the disciples said to Jesus in Luke 10:17 et seq.; "Lord, the devils also are subject to us in thy name", they were told: "I saw Satan like lightning falling from heaven." When St. Paul calls upon Christians to put on the armour of God so as to resist the attacks of the devil, he explains that they have to fight, not against "flesh and blood", but "against principalities and powers, against the rulers of the world of this darkness, against the spirits of wickedness in the high places" (Eph. 6:11 et seq.). According to Apoc. 12:9 Satan was cast to earth with his angels, and in Apoc. 16:13 et seq., he (and Antichrist) emits three unclean spirits from his mouth. These passages show that the numerous powers all derive from one fundamental power, which is called Satan; they may be regarded as emanations and effects of that power

[20] Matt. 9:34; 25:41.

16

which is manifest in theirs. In them we encounter outpourings of Satan's power. That is the significance of the name ἡ δύναμις τοῦ ἐχθροῦ, "the power of the enemy" (Luke 10:19): it is in them and through them that Satan's influence operates. All the devil's power meets in their multiplicity.

We have seen so far that in the principalities and powers mentioned in the New Testament a phenomenon is being glimpsed which obtrudes intensively upon all men, and especially upon Christians. This phenomenon is described by numerous names which the New Testament has borrowed from other sources. The use of so many names indicates that the subject is not adequately described by any one name. Fundamentally, we are dealing with a single phenomenon which is diffused, and which concerns us in various manifestations.

This is not all there is to be gathered from an examination of the names of these powers. But first let us remember that St. Paul tells us in the Epistle to the Ephesians that these principalities have their abode, and presumably also their being, in "the high places".[21] These places are not heaven, where God is. They signify the "heavens" which surround and touch upon the material world and provide the dimensions in which everything material is contained. Man's earthly existence is directed towards it; it is the transcendence towards which the man of "flesh and blood" always tends. By the heavens we mean the supreme form of material life; it is the Unseen which we nevertheless perceive, and which passes into infinity. It is the human heavens from which man and his world live, by which he is

---

[21] On τὰ ἐπουράνια see H. Schlier, *Der Brief an die Epheser* (1957), pp. 45–8.

menaced, seduced and determined. That is the essential abode of the principalities. And since they live in this world and operate through it, they are part of the "invisible" things which are mentioned in Col. 1:16. The invisible is the supreme form of the material; the principalities are phenomena of the invisible in this sense, and, as such, their nature has a double characteristic which seems self-contradictory to us, although we know it by experience.

The New Testament teaches on the one hand that the demoniacal powers are a kind of personal beings. Precisely that is immediately obvious from the names which they bear; as we have already seen, they are called gods, princes, and angels. Satan is the prince of this world and the god of the world, as well as the accuser, the tempter, the adversary, and the destroyer. The same point emerges, as we shall see, from what we are told about the operations of Satan and of the principalities.

But what is meant by "personal being"? It means that they manifest themselves as beings of intellect and will, which can speak and be spoken to. They are something which is capable of purposeful activity.

But they are not always encountered as individuals. Sometimes they are examples of a species. The demon (almost always τὸ δαιμόνιον, like τὸ θεῖον[22]), in the New Testament sense is a specimen of what is demoniacal. For example, the man of Gerasa in Mark 5:1 et seq., was possessed by one δαιμόνιον. His name, by which he makes himself known and perceived, is said to be "Legion, for we are many". Here one is many and many are one. The same idea is also expressed in the term

---

[22] Cf. for example, Plato, *Republic,* II 382 e; ThWB, II, 9, note 63.

Pneuma, used in the singular and in the plural, and it is suggested even more in the phrase τὰ πνευματικὰ τῆς πονηρίας in Eph. 6:12 that the principalities and powers are representatives of a collective principle. In them a collective spirit of evil is at work.

This brings us to the other aspect. These principalities are not only a kind of personal beings, examples of a comprehensible species of beings with will and intelligence, but also beings of power. In this context the word "being" is to be understood both as a verb and as a noun. Not all of their titles show that they are beings of power; but we have already established that their names are generally interchangeable, so that whatever applies to one applies to others also.

Two passages are of importance in this connection: Eph. 1:21: Christ is above "all principality (ἀρχὴ) and power (ἐξουσία) and virtue (δύναμις) and dominion (κυριότης) and every name (ὄνομα) that is named" (cf. Col. 1:16).

Another passage is Rom. 8:38: "For I am sure that neither death, nor life, nor angels, nor principalities, nor powers, nor things present, nor things to come, nor might, nor height, nor depth, nor any other creature, shall be able to separate us from the love of God which is in Christ Jesus our Lord."

From these passages we learn that, as well as being personal beings in the sense explained above, they are also "power", "might", etc. They do not merely possess power and the other attributes, they are power. They are not just something or somebody, and also have power. They exist as power, etc. That is what they are called, and they get these names because that is how they manifest themselves and their being.

And that is why – as we see in these passages – St. Paul

enumerates them in the same breath with such phenomena as life, present, future, height, and depth. Evidently while they are powers of existence, dominating, embracing, determining powers, they have something in common with these other enumerated phenomena. That common element is their nature as power, as threatening superior power.

This point emerges even more·clearly from 1 Cor. 15:23–26, where "death" is singled out as the last of the enemies which Christ shall destroy. These enemies are πᾶσα ἀρχὴ καὶ πᾶσα ἐξουσία καὶ δύναμις. So indeed the principalities do not merely possess power; they are power, or at any rate it is as power that they exist. And they are pure power, not merely the power of the universe as such; they are powers pure and simple, not the power of space, time or existence in general, or of the void. They are power, capacity, dominion in person;[23] they are the personified essence of power, capacity etc.

This definition may somehow cover the contradictory descriptions of their nature apparent in their names. But perhaps our definition is too wide. It would be more exact to say that their being is the being of an intelligent will which has power and aims at power; it is the being of a "will-power" and also of a "power-will". We have here a multiple manifestation of an invisible power which comes from the limit of the natural order, where it abides. The New Testament calls it "spirit". The word denotes a being of personal power, such as the being of

---

[23] These beings can make themselves felt in a very concrete manner, but the abstract way in which they were imagined is well illustrated in the apocryphal *Acts of John,* c. 99, p. 200, 13 et seq., which speaks of virtues, powers, principalities, demons, energies (ἐνέργειαι), menaces (ἀπειλαί), tempers (θυμοί), devil, Satan and the lower root.

the demoniacal powers is. As we have seen, this is made quite clear, not only in the popular narratives and thought of the Synoptic Gospels, but also in theological texts of the New Testament.

These considerations shed some light on the phenomenon with which we are dealing. But what we have achieved so far is very much a matter of formal, almost empty terminology. These powers have revealed themselves as manifestations of a spirit which is a person. We may learn a little more about their nature by enquiring what they do. We might also ask in what manner these powers possess their nature. The immediate and unanimous answer is that they possess it in such a way as to influence the world and men, thereby displaying their powerful nature to and through men. A few examples will illustrate our meaning.

We begin with happenings which are frequently reported in the Synoptic Gospels. Time and again we are told about human beings under the influence of an "unclean" or a "wicked" spirit. This "spirit" or "demon" shows its nature by producing bodily or spiritual maladies of a somewhat indeterminate kind. Thus St. Luke (13:11) tells us: "There was a woman, who had a spirit of infirmity eighteen years: and she was bowed together, neither could she look upwards at all." Jesus describes the woman as "this daughter of Abraham, whom Satan hath bound these eighteen years" (Luke 13:16). In another case St. Matthew (12:22) speaks of "one possessed with a devil, blind and dumb".

It is often suggested that these expressions, and others like them, are merely the explanations which primitive medicine offered for ailments such as blindness and dumbness. But this

21

is not the case. These expressions draw attention to what underlies the fact of illness. No matter what physical or psychic causes it may have, illness also is due to a superior evil power. The incidence of illness may seem fortuitous to men, but it is due to the calculated action of the superior wicked power: though this action is deliberate, man cannot predict it. This superior power has its being, not only in the impairment of the body, but also in the confusion and ruin of the spirit.

In so-called spiritual or mental illness, and in maladies close to it such as epilepsy,[24] we perceive an element of "possession", that in a wider sense underlies all maladies. This is true even today, when our advanced medical knowledge is still perplexed by the ultimate cause of mental illness.

There are three characteristic expressions in the New Testament for those suffering from spiritual maladies. In Mark 1:23, one is called ἄνθρωπος ἐν πνεύματι ἀκαθάρτῳ. Another description is δαιμονιζόμενος (Matthew 8:28), δαιμονίσθεις (Mark 5:18), ἐνοχλούμενος or ἐνοχλούμενος ὑπὸ (or ἀπὸ) πνευμάτων ἀκαθάρτων (Luke 6:18; Acts 5:16). A third term is ἔχων δαιμόνια (Luke 8:27). He who is spiritually ill thus has a demon, or a number of them. The "unclean spirit" has taken possession of him and has taken up its abode in the man, in his body and in his soul. He has done so in such a way that we might, conversely, regard the unclean spirit as the abode in which the patient resides. Thus a passage such as Mark 9:24 refers to the "spirit" "entering into" (ἐισελθεῖν) a man, in order to reveal to the man that the unclean spirit is now the ambience in which he lives, and by living in which he disintegrates. The demon

---

[24] Mark 9:14 et seq.; 2 Cor. 12:7.

fulfills his function of being the ruin and destruction of creation,[25] when he takes possession of the man from within and undoes him, so as to enclose him within the compass of his power.

We also learn from the New Testament that man is not the only victim of the evil powers. It is also part of their nature to influence nature so as to enhance their claims and authority over man.

In the fourth Chapter of the Epistle to the Galatians, St. Paul warns his readers against relapsing into an understanding of God and a relationship with him based on the demands of the Jewish Law. He here reminds them of the form in which the demands of the Law had been proposed to them when they were Gentiles: the instruction which they received in their anxiety had given them "the weak and needy elements" (στοιχεῖα). These "elements" are probably the stars under whose influence the Galatians had felt bound to observe certain sidereal festivals. The stars are, of course, works of the Creator, and they may be studied in the spirit of the Book of Wisdom. But in this context they are considered as influences whose power and spirit is felt, as gods "who, by nature, are not gods" (Gal. 4:8). The principalities which dominate the stars, make them as it were "gods", or as Paul says in Col. 2:18, "angels" or "principalities and powers" (Col. 2:10–15). More accurately, we might say that in this way these principalities let their influence be felt.

Thus, through those stars and, of course, through other elements of which they have taken possession, the principalities exercise their ominous "influence". They exploit the law which governs these elements by imposing upon the pagans their

---

[25] Possession by an unclean spirit can even go so far that the man identifies himself with the spirit, as we see from Mark 5:6 et seq.

own fiendish law. Thereby they ensure that the pagans also fall under the perverted law which spells death. As they resemble the element so closely, it is as "elements" that they themselves have come to be known.

Even the circumstances of history fall under this influence, and historical institutions and situations have thus become place and location, means and instruments of those powers. We have in mind here such statements as St. Paul's declaration in 1 Thess. 2:18, that Satan twice hindered him from bringing consolation to the Thessalonians in their distress. In that case, Satan had arranged certain circumstances and situations, in which and through which he worked. Again the meaning of Rom. 8:35, may well be that the inherent distresses of this life which press upon the world are due to the powers which he mentions in Rom. 8:38. It is in the same light that John, the seer of the Apocalypse, views the situation in Smyrna, where Christians are being persecuted: "Behold, the devil will cast some of you into prison" (Apoc. 2:10).

But above all we are thinking of chapter 13 of the Apocalypse which draws a sinister picture of the exploitation of public and political life, its organs and persons, by the satanic spirit which perverts them. Here we are provided with a concrete answer to the question of how these principalities have their nature. We are told that the dragon gave the beast from the sea "his own strength and great power" (Apoc. 12:9). Satan has assumed the image of the dragon; the beast is the apocalyptic image of the anti-Christian *imperium*. Satan exercises his power by lending it to the political powers, in order that they, by governing against Christ, may manifest and exercise it. "The dwellers on the earth", as mankind is called, adore the "beast", which is the animal nature of the anti-Christian state, and they cry enthusiastically: "Who is like to the beast? And who shall be able to fight with him?", for the beast has superlative military strength as well as indestructible vital power. By doing this they adore in reality the "dragon" which "gave power to the beast" (Apoc. 13:4).

But in what way has he given the beast power by which and in what it can live? The seer observes yet another beast "coming up out of the earth": this second beast causes the first to speak, to do and to be what it is by virtue of the dragon. Evidently this second beast is the incarnation of the spirit which makes the first beast manifest the nature which it has received from Satan's power. That is why the second beast speaks "as a dragon" (Apoc. 13:11), and executes "all the power of the former beast in his (the dragon's) sight" (Apoc. 13:12). In Apoc. 13:13 et seq., we are told that it uses signs and wonders to move "them that dwell on the earth" to make an image of the first beast. It causes the anti-Christian state to be projected into, and seen as, an idol. The beast constructs a political philosophy, an ideology, by means of which the authority of this state permeates everything, establishes itself and operates in all places. As the seer says: "It was given to him (the second beast) to give life to the image of the (first) beast: and that the image of the beast should speak; and should cause that whosoever will not adore the image of the beast should be slain" (13:15). In itself such a political philosophy is inert and inactive. It becomes articulate when it asserts its claims through physical force, and produces terror and fear. The power of Satan finds its own in the totalitarian anti-Christian rule which compels all those who dwell on the earth "both little and great,

25

rich and poor, freemen and bondmen, to have a character on their right hand or on their foreheads: and that no man might buy or sell, but he that hath the character, or the name of the beast, or the number of his name" (Apoc. 13:16 et seq.). The totalitarian anti-Christian state wipes out all distinctions among men, except between friends and enemies of the dominant régime. Those bearing the mark of the new, metaphysical, slavery are separated and marked off from those who reject it at the risk of their lives. The totalitarian spirit gathers the servile élite of the state party, and so it can withdraw the most elementary means of livelihood from the opponents of Satan's dominion, who are declared public enemies. This division of mankind enables the ruling apparatus to become absolute and supreme. Satan can thus take possession of public life by so filling the persons, means and organs of government with the will to power, that it inspires them to perform vicious actions, and invests that spirit with its deadly effectiveness.

But the religious sphere too can be seized by that being of intelligent lust for power. It penetrates the world and the hearts of men through the pagan gods, the Jewish Law, and Christian heresies, which it has already influenced. St. Paul says in 1 Cor. 10:19 et seq., that a Christian, who, on the invitation of a pagan friend partakes of the sacrifice and the sacred meal in honour of the god Serapis, thereby aligns himself with the devils who lurk behind the pagan cults. It is true, as Paul himself says in 1 Cor. 8:5, that they merely "are called gods", and that they "by nature, are not gods" (Gal. 4:8): there is no divine being except God. Nevertheless, when the pagans acknowledge these gods, they acquire a "demoniacal" authority, and this authority draws power from the spirit which leads the pagans to such worship. It is a power which subdues even the man who knows that in reality they are nothing. This power at any rate fascinated the pagans. The Corinthians were reminded in 1 Cor. 12:2 that "when you were heathens, you went to dumb idols, according as you were led". Even Christians are not immune from the influence of these dumb idols if they venture near them, for though the idols are nothing, the demons control them. The "demoniacal" power of these idols is so great that, according to Apoc. 9:20, "the rest of the men, who were not slain by these plagues, did not do penance from the works of their hands, that they should not adore devils, and idols of gold, and silver, and brass, and stone, and wood, which neither can see, nor hear, nor walk".

Indeed, according to St. Paul, the influence of the wicked angels is asserted even in the Jewish Law, that had ceased to be understood in the original sense of God's appeal to it. In the hands of fallen men even the "holy, and just, and good" commandment (Rom. 7:12) becomes a Law which fosters self-seeking and self-advancement. To this extent the fallen angels speak through the Law, and it conveys the words of the Evil One who tries to master men by secretly and subtly exploiting their self-seeking and self-righteousness.[26] So the influence of evil powers has a most intimate effect on the claims and dealings of everyday human life.

The same picture appears in the Gospel of St. John, where the Jews are the prototype of infidels who reject Jesus and his truth. And Jesus says of them: "You are of your father the devil:

[26] This point is fully developed in H. Schlier, *Der Brief an die Galater* (1953), pp. 104 et seq.

and the desires of your father will you do" (John 8:44). And in Apoc. 2:9 the Jewish synagogue is revealed as the "synagogue of Satan" who uses the Jews to persecute Christians.

Finally, there is yet another manner in which the evil power exercises its nature: its spirit influences even Christian revelation. St. Paul has this in mind when he speaks of "false apostles . . . transforming themselves into the apostles of Christ". He continues: "And no wonder: for Satan himself transformeth himself into an angel of light. Therefore it is no great thing if his ministers be transformed as the ministers of justice" (2 Cor. 11:13–15). Again in 1 Tim. 4:1 he says: "Now the Spirit manifestly saith that in the last times some shall depart from the faith, giving heed to spirits of error and doctrines of devils." The first epistle of St. John issues a similar warning against false Christian prophets who are inspired by the spirit of Antichrist: "Believe not every spirit" (John 4:1). The Epistle of St. James distinguishes between "wisdom from above" and "earthly, sensual, devilish" wisdom (Jas. 3:15). Christian heresy may be described as the wisdom of Christian teaching when penetrated by the spirit of evil. Even Christian doctrine can be exploited by the evil spirit.

Thus, according to the New Testament teaching, Satan and his hordes, those manifold developments and effusions of the spirit of wickedness with their combination of intelligence and lust for power, exist by influencing the world and mankind in every sector and at all levels, and by making them instruments and bearers of their power. There is nothing on earth which is absolutely immune from their power. They can occupy the human body, the human spirit, what we call "nature", and even the forms, bearers and situations of history. Even religions, including the Christian teaching, can become tools of their activity. Their spirit penetrates and overwhelms everything.

At this point there is one observation to be made. When the principalities penetrate the world and the circumstances of human life in order to exercise their power through them, they thereby conceal themselves in the world and in the every-day life of mankind. They withdraw from sight into the men, elements, and institutions through which they make their power felt. To seem not to appear is part of their essence. When the loyal citizen of Pergamus looked up at his Acropolis, he saw above him, and unquestioningly accepted, the temple of Augustus and Roma. But the seer of the Apocalypse could tell the Church of Pergamus: "I know where thou dwellest, where the seat of Satan is" (Apoc. 2:13). He saw more than the citizen. The temple of the gods was there to be seen: but the seer looked beyond it and perceived the satanic power which operated in and through this temple. This power was hidden, but it was no less active in spite of its concealment.

Indeed these powers conceal their presence to such an extent that, as we have seen, even their names are concealed. The Greek word στοιχεῖα means the elements, such as the stars, but it is also applied to the powers who lie hidden in these elements, and who operate from their concealment. To the superficial mind they will always be merely natural elements, but that is an abstraction from reality. For in the reality of their historical appearance these elements – and indeed nature in general – are subject either to the claims of God, or to those of the devil. But of course this claim lies hidden in them.

Their hidden nature, which is their main characteristic, according to the New Testament is still more effective

29

because the reason for their presence remains impenetrable for man. No man knows why they single out any particular person, circumstance or time for exercising their influence. No human eye can discern why some havoc has been wrought, when and why it ceases, into what it is being transformed. This spirit covers the world with a great shroud of mystery, under which there is a perpetual disturbance, continuous unrest. Seeming clarification may be followed by sudden gloom, there may be astounding interventions, strange renunciations: these phenomena only serve to withdraw the spirit from man's understanding and grasp, demonstrating only the superior power of a transcendent spirit over which he has no control.

There is a passage in St. Paul which further illustrates what has been said, at least in regard to some of the principalities. In the Epistle to the Ephesians 2:2, "the prince of this world" is called "the prince of the power of this air". This strange name implies that the air is the medium in which his power is exercised. St. Paul is here in line with ancient tradition, particularly the statements of late Judaism.[27] But what does he mean by "the air"? Paul himself provides the answer to this question: he explains that it is "the spirit that now worketh on the children of unbelief" – that is, on men who have rejected the Gospel. This is a helpful interpretation, for it shows that Satan's influence over the world enables him to control the spirit which dominates unbelievers. But what is this spirit? In this context at least, it is the universal spirit of man's unbelief or disobedience.

[27] See for example: *Testament of XII Patriarchs,* Benj. 3:2; Henoch 5 (Rec A); Philo, *Gig* 6; *Plant* 14; *Conf. ling.,* p. 174 et seq.; *Asc. Jes.* 10, 29 et seq.; Papyrus-Berlin 5025 (= Preisendanz, *Pap. Mag.* I, 215). See also H. Schlier, *Der Brief an die Epheser* (1957), pp. 101 et seq.

It is the general spiritual climate which influences mankind, in which men live, which they breathe, which dominates their thoughts, aspirations, and deeds. He exercises his "influence" over men by means of the spiritual atmosphere which he dominates and uses as the medium for his power. He gains power over men and penetrates them by means of this atmosphere, which is his realm, the realm of his power. If men expose themselves to this atmosphere, they become its carriers, and thereby contribute to its extension.

But this atmosphere is not the only realm or means of his domination. As we have seen, he takes possession of all levels of natural everyday life; he attacks it at every possible level, in the soul and body of the individual or in what we call natural phenomena. Moreover, the atmosphere is not the only dimension in which he operates, and hence this spiritual domination is not his only weapon. Quite apart from the physical harm of which the spiritual domination is capable, Satan can inflict bodily harm without using spiritual domination as his medium. But the atmosphere is the principal source of his domination. At any rate St. Paul regards it as the chief means by which the principalities exercise their domination. This domination usually begins in the general spirit of the world, or in the spirit of a particular period, attitude, nation or locality. This spirit, in which the "course of this world" rules, is not just floating about freely. Men inhale it and thus pass it on into their institutions and various conditions. In certain situations it becomes concentrated. Indeed, it is so intense and powerful that no individual can escape it. It serves as a norm and is taken for granted. To act, think or speak against this spirit is regarded as non-sensical or even as wrong and criminal. It is "in" this

31

spirit that men encounter the world and affairs, which means that they accept the world as this spirit presents it to them, with all its ideas and values, in the form in which he wants them to find it. The domination which the prince of this world exercises over the atmosphere, gives to the world with its affairs, relationships and situations, and even to existence itself, the appearance of belonging to him; it imposes his valuation on everything.

This brings us to the heart of what is to be said about the nature of the powers. We have just described the kind and manner of their nature. They present and interpret everything in the universe which they dominate in their own light and in their own way. It is their nature to invest men, the elements, the circumstances and institutions of life, even the spiritual realities – in short everything natural or human, under their dominion, with an appearance of their own making. It is their nature to interpret the universe and human existence in their own way. This interpretation implies not only that they cause things to happen in a particular perspective, but also to be encountered in a particular state. To interpret is not merely to imagine, but also to create in a particular way; it is an indivisible process. Interpretation as revealing representation is the nature of spirit as such, it is also the nature of the spirit with which we are now dealing. An interpretation of this kind will for instance invest idols, which indeed are "nothing", with the fascination of supremely powerful beings. Some uncanny and numinous quality imbues the very form of idols and emanates from them. Such interpretation also causes stars to appear as gods or angels, and as such to assert claims to which men succumb. Such interpretation will also give rise to the totalitarian state with its institutions, claims and actions, and their inhuman consequences and effects. Ultimately such interpretation will cause the individual to misunderstand himself and his world, and thereby to be utterly ruined.

But what is the intention of the powers in their presentation and remodelling of reality? The answer emerges when we consider the kind of reality of the universe and of human existence that their interpretation presents.

In their nature the principalities present the universe and human life as a world of death. It is by subjecting them that death results. Through their nature they introduce death to the world, and so they show themselves as beings of death.

In St. Mark's Gospel 5:1 et seq., this is very vividly expressed in that strange story of the healing of the possessed in the land of the Gerasenes or Gadarenes. The man possessed by the "unclean spirit" has a compulsory affinity to death. Not only does he dwell in the desert among tombs, in the place of death, and is tormented by the release which Jesus is about to bring him, because he is content with his ruined world and life; he also has an inner urge to self-destruction and to the destruction of his environment. The "unclean spirit" which controls him from within, shows itself clearly as the spirit of death.

Many other stories of the Synoptic Gospels also confirm the tendency of the satanic power to be the distortion, thwarting, ruin, annihilation, and undoing of creation.

The same point emerges also in a wholly different field. The Apocalypse, chapter 12 et seq., deals with the nature of Satan – the dragon – and of the total political power which he inspires. His nature is revealed in his ultimate aim; this aim, as we have seen, is boycott, persecution, captivity, war and death.

33

That is why he is called in 1 Cor. 10:10 "the destroyer", but in John 8:44 Jesus can say explicitly that "he was a murderer from the beginning". Thus it is he who inspires hatred, and thereby causes the death both of the one who hates – who hates in fear of Satan – and of him who is hated, whom Satan assails through hatred. This point is developed in 1 John 3:7–12. When men consider death as the last and supreme power, this is due to the devil, who thereby causes fear which leads to hatred. Satan's nature operates by making the universe and all existence appear as a universe and an existence of death, an encounter in anxiety and woes. We are told in Heb. 2:14–15 that he has "the empire of death": that is how he holds men "all their lifetime subject to servitude" through "the fear of death".

But the evil principalities also try to present the universe and existence, in general and in particular matters, as temptation. Because of the interpreting spirit of evil the whole fullness of ever-changing life – and death – appears enticing and menacing. The actions and speech of men, their gestures, their thinking and their bearing; their very situations, elementary forces and intellectual movements are affected in this way. This enticement and menace ultimately has an absolute character and the object of causing the fall of man, that is, his withdrawal and falling away from God. This is illustrated by the miracles of Antichrist, which are described in Apoc. 13:13 et seq.: these miracles are primarily feats of a technical and social nature and have for men the power and the glamour of temptations. But distress and persecution too can have the effects of temptation upon them.[28] Both favourable and unfavourable factors, decline as

---

[28] 1 Thess. 3:5; Luke 22:31; Apoc. 2:10 etc.

well as increase of life, are the devil's means to assert his nature. He is the "tempter"[29] as such. Temptation is his inner-most nature. In the temptation of mankind he fulfils his enmity against God. Through temptation he leads men to sin. The New Testament (Eph. 2:2 et seq.) shows that in this respect to sin is to live according to the standard of that spirit which makes the world and life in the world appear eternal. Sin occurs through man's self-willed greed for the world and through his acceptance of the world which the devil conjures up as the ultimate ground and object of existence. That is the meaning of 1 John 3:8 (cf. 5:18): "He that committeth sin is of the devil: for the devil sinneth from the beginning." To succumb to the world-reality presented by the devil temptingly either as eternal joy or eternal death, is to assent to his will and its life therefrom; the devil proving himself to be the "whence", the principle of sin. Indeed, when St. Paul is thinking of the con-nection between sin and the devil, "sin" itself appears as a power.[30] It will be remembered that the same is true of death, which is explicitly reckoned among the powers in 1 Cor. 15:26, where it is called the last enemy.

In such a seductive design of the world, another essential quality of the spirit of evil – falsehood – is at work. Falsehood is the deliberate deceiving and distorting presentation of reality in and through this spirit. Jesus says of the devil: "When he speaketh a lie, he speaketh of his own: for he is a liar" (John 8:44). St. Paul tells us in 2 Cor. 11:14 that Satan falsely changes into an angel of light in order to deceive men. Thus Satan's nature

---

[29] 1 Thess. 3:5; Matt. 4:3; 1 Peter 5:8; Acts 20:19; Apoc. 3:10.
[30] See, for example, Rom. 5:12, 21; 6:1, 7, 12, 13; 7:7 et seq.

is also falsehood. Even as destroyer and tempter his nature is falsehood, for the death which he brings, and the world which he presents, are falsehood. But this is not all. He attaches great value to illumination and speaks much of it; but the only illumination which he provides is to spread a deceptive semblance over reality, surrounding it with an aura of deceit; this he may accomplish by conjuring up deliberate and calculated illusions by means of the "spirits of devils" from the mouth of the dragon and of the anti-Christian State, in order to move the "kings of the whole earth" (Apoc. 16:14) into war against God. He also operates through heresy (1 Tim. 4:1; 2 Tim. 2:26), and generally through causing "all seduction of error" on the part of the Antichrist (1 Thess, 2:9 et seq.). And everywhere the very illumination which the nature of Satan produces is really the establishment of the power of darkness, the ἐξουσία τοῦ σκότους (Acts 26:18; Col. 1:13), in which men shall live, or rather shall die.

Finally, Satan is described in the New Testament, as "the accuser (ὁ κατήγωρ or κατήγορος) of our brethren . . . who accused them before our God day and night" (Apoc. 12:10). This description, which occurs in the Old Testament (Job 1:6 et seq.; Zach. 3:1 et seq.), and in Jewish literature,[31] also indicates a tendency of his nature. This tendency is of course not operative, as it were, in addition to destroying, tempting, and deceiving, but is included in them. It reveals the depth of the other tendencies, and their actual aim. The distorting interpretation of things leading to sin unto death becomes a lying and deadly accusation before God of seduced mankind. The

[31] See Strack-Billerbeck I, pp. 141 et seq.

36

devilish tone of the accusation is provided by the deceptive interpretation the world and of mankind designed to draw man from God and to subject him to death. Human life, deluded by the devil and thereby becoming self-centered and subject to death, appears in this way as absolute guilt.

There is one final point in this connection which is decisive for an understanding of the nature of these powers. According to the New Testament, these powers too were originally creatures of God, and part of the reality which God called into being, of Creation. As St. Paul says in Rom. 8:38: "I am sure that neither death, nor life, nor angels, nor principalities, nor powers, nor things present, nor things to come, nor might, nor height, nor depth, nor *any other creature* (κτίσις), shall be able to separate us from the love of God, which is in Christ Jesus our Lord": and in Col. 1:16 he adds that God created the principalities, "visible and invisible", in and through Christ and with Christ as their object, and having their being in him. Thus these principalities owe their being to God. Their origin too is in Christ, and through him and for him. Their source and their final end is not in themselves, but in Jesus Christ, who is God.

It follows that in origin, and in the source of their being, the principalities are good. They too indicate that, according to the New Testament, power as such is not evil, but good. Power as such is not in opposition to God's will, but proceeds from, and conforms to, it. This was first denied by the Gnostics and Manichaeans.

But this is where the nature of these principalities is revealed: that they no longer exist as that which they are. They present themselves now having discarded their divine origin, and become autonomous. As powers they come from God; but as they now appear, they are their own source.

The New Testament touches briefly on this fact in one passage of the short Epistle of St. Jude (verse 6), one of the later and lesser known writings; there we are told that "the angels . . . kept not their principality but forsook their own habitation". The reference here is to the so-called fall of the angels, which is also mentioned in the related Epistle of St. Peter (2 Peter 2:4), and was known in different variations to Jewish tradition.[32] What exactly is conveyed by this fall of the angels? It is conveyed that God has ordained and assigned a position of power for these angels – the principalities – which they no longer exercise, nor do they occupy the locality where God had placed them. As a result of a mysterious desire for creatures they have become independent and autonomous, ego-centric and self-willed. Their dominion they still owe to God; even the devil has his power and *is* power because of God. But this power now operates as if it were self-ordained. He now has an autonomous nature. He and all the principalities now maintain as their own that which was given to them by God.

Thus their nature now is autonomous self-centredness; a self-centredness, however, that is in opposition to God and God's power. It is part of their nature to be against God. The devil is the "wicked one", the "adversary", and the "enemy",[33] because of the opposition to God of the devil's self-seeking and self-willed independent and autonomous nature. For rebellion

[32] See 1 Enoch 6 et seq.; 9:4 et seq.; 10:11 et seq.; 12:4; 15:3; 19:4; 2 Enoch 18:4 et seq.; Jub. 4:22; 5:1 et seq.; 10; syr Bar 56:10 et seq.; Test. XII Patr., Ruben, 5; Philo, Gig. 2; Jos. Ant. 1, 3, 1; Pirqe R El 13 27; Sanh. 38 b.

[33] Matt. 13:19; 6:13; John 17:15; Eph. 6:16; 2 Thess. 3:3; 1 John 2:13, 14; 5:18; 1 Peter 5:8; Matt. 13:25, 28, 39; Luke 10:19; Acts 13:10.

against God is expressed in all the tendencies and methods of such a being, in his "interpretation" of the world and its life which he has made his own, in his destruction, temptation, distortion, and accusation.

II

JESUS CHRIST AND THE PRINCIPALITIES

THE principalities, virtues and powers, the spirit of wickedness and its emanations, which continuously struggle to obtain dominion over the world and mankind, have been overcome by Jesus Christ and condemned by him to await the final ruin of their power. The triumph of Christ over the principalities is a frequent theme in the New Testament. It forms an essential part of the teaching of the apostles.

St. Matthew and St. Luke place the story of our Lord's temptation at the beginning of his public life; St. Mark briefly refers to it.[34] It was the aim of the evangelists to impress upon the community what tradition taught, that this Jesus Christ, of whom the whole Gospel tells, faced the devil and overcame him before he did anything else.

The first undisguised encounter between the Son of God and the spirit of wickedness took place in the desert. Through the unwavering obedience of the Son to the Father, all that was revealed in that encounter was the nature of this spirit as temptation and self-glory. Only the powerlessness of this self-glory before unfailing obedience to God was exhibited. After that episode the Gospel shows us Jesus Christ as the Son of God who has already achieved a decisive victory over the spirit of self-

[34] Matt. 4:1–11; Luke 4:1–13; Mark 1:12–13.

glorifying, seductive power, in order now in words and deed to continue this victory among men and for them, and to accomplish it on the cross.

It is in this way also that the evangelists and their tradition understood and presented the work of Jesus on earth as an unwearying and uninterrupted struggle between Jesus and the powerful spirit of evil roused as it were before him, and as a continual victory over it to be achieved – not without fresh and special temptations. This is illustrated by a statement of Jesus to the disciples, which also shows the humanity of the Son of God: "You are they who have continued with me in my temptations" (Luke 22:28). An echo of this tradition is to be found in the Epistle to the Hebrews 4:15: "We have not a high priest who cannot have compassion on our infirmities: but one tempted in all things like as we are, without sin."[35]

The Synoptic Gospels record many exorcisms which Jesus performed and which show in detail his struggle against the powerful spirit of wickedness. It is also mentioned in their occasional short summaries of the activity of Jesus, for instance in Mark 1:32 et seq.: "And when it was evening, after sunset, they brought to him all that were ill and that were possessed with devils. And all the city was gathered together at the door. And he healed many that were troubled with divers diseases. And he cast out many devils: and he suffered them not to speak, because they knew him." The Gospel of St. Luke contains a summing up of his work by Jesus himself: "Behold, I cast out devils and do cures, today and tomorrow, and the third day I

[35] See also 2:17 et seq. (5:2).

41

am consummated" (13:32).[36] This is echoed by an ancient tradition preserved in Acts 10:38: "Jesus of Nazareth: how God anointed him with the Holy Ghost and with power, who went about doing good and healing all that were oppressed by the devil, for God was with him."

The large number of possessed persons in Judaea and Galilee at that time has often been noted and is, indeed, striking. It has sometimes been explained as a deliberate exaggeration by the evangelists. But the gospels themselves can account for the frequency of cases of possession. The spirit of self-glorification perceived the arrival of the perfectly obedient Jesus to be a challenge and indictment of itself. This is made clear in one of the so-called "paradigmatic" narratives, which also relates how Jesus defeated the demons. For example, Mark. 1:21–8 tells us:

"And they entered into Capharnaum: and forthwith upon the sabbath days going into the synagogue, he taught them. And they were astonished at his doctrine. For he was teaching them as one having power, and not as the scribes. And there was in their synagogue a man with an unclean spirit; and he cried out, saying: What have we to do with thee, Jesus of Nazareth? Art thou come to destroy us? I know who thou art, the Holy One of God. And Jesus threatened him, saying: Speak no more, and go out of the man. And the unclean spirit, tearing him and crying out with a loud voice, went out of him. And they were all amazed, insomuch that they questioned among themselves, saying: What is this new doctrine? For with power he commandeth even the unclean spirits: and they obey him."

The simple story shows that where Jesus appears, imparting

---

[36] See also 11:20 = Matt. 12:27.

with authority the "new" teaching (and not teaching like the Pharisees), he who is possessed by the unclean spirit must come too. Without this being said explicitly, it is the word of Jesus that draws him. But the demon in the possessed man at once feels himself threatened by the presence of Jesus. He instantly perceives a danger to himself and senses his own ruin in Jesus and in the spirit of the "Holy One of God", as he himself calls him. We are reminded of the cry of the two possessed creatures from the country of the Gerasenes: "What dost have we to do with thee, Jesus Son of God? Art thou come hither to torment us *before the time?*" (Matt. 8:29). The evil spirit perceives, as it were, the End, the ultimate judgement which, in the person of Jesus, has broken upon the world and which spells doom for the self-willed spirit of destruction. In the face of this threat he reveals himself as being subject to time and, therefore, powerless, although indeed to the end he will try to camouflage himself and to hold on to his power: "The unclean spirit tearing him and crying out with a loud voice, went out of him" (verse 26). From the outset Jesus is his master. Jesus not only knows of him, but commands him and drives him out – "and they obey him" (verse 27).

So much may be learned from this story. But we may ask; by what power does Jesus command the spirits? St. Luke, who records the same event as St. Mark, has the bystanders wondering: "What word is this, for with authority and power (ἐν ἐξουσίᾳ καὶ δυνάμει) he commandeth the unclean spirits and they go out?" The gospel tradition shows that it is the word of the power of God which Jesus exercises when he speaks.[37] Jesus

---

[37] See Luke 9:43.

himself said (Luke 11:20): "I, by the finger of God, cast out devils"; St. Matthew 12:28, writes "by the Spirit of God".

But how does Jesus in his powerful word exercise the power of God which drives out devils, and the Spirit of God which banishes the demons? We answer that he receives this power from God, and exercises it by prayer and obedience to God. "All things are possible to him that believeth", and "this kind can go out by nothing but prayer and fasting" (Mark 9:22, 28).

Obedience to God implies to be given over to men; this is the foundation of the power to which the demons yield. Obedience is always the root of pity and love for men for the sake of God. Jesus said: "O incredulous generation, how long shall I be with you? How long shall I suffer you?" (Mark 9:18). St. Matthew had the same idea in mind when he wrote: "When evening was come, they brought to him many that were possessed by devils: and he cast out the spirits with his word: and all that were sick he healed: that it might be fulfilled which was spoken by the prophet Isaias, saying: He took our infirmities and bore our diseases" (Matt. 8:16 et seq.). The demons flee before the word of command which lays them bare; this word comes from him who, as the promised servant of God, takes upon himself even the effects of their actions as a weakness and disease of men, and embraces them in his passion. The power of evil, the nature of autonomy, the ruinous influence of the pride of the spirit, dissolve and yield before the mighty word of the love of Jesus, who in obedience to God, takes upon himself and bears even these beings for the sake of mankind.

This selfless love of Jesus for God and (under God's direction) for man, which overcomes the spirit of self-glory, was accomplished according to the Gospels, and the whole apostolic tradition, on the cross of Jesus. In the passion and death which the demons and the men subservient to them prepared for Jesus Christ, the proud power of Satan was rendered impotent. Dying with the body of Christ on the cross is all the self-righteousness of men, and the spirit of self-glory which possesses them. On the cross the power of the principalities was shattered by the unbreakable power of love.[38] That this love did not end in death we know from Jesus Christ's resurrection from the dead, when he was "exalted" above "all principality and power". In Jesus Christ, obedient to God in his resurrection, ascension and glorification, the power of God triumphs over all principalities.

This is repeatedly stressed by St. John and St. Paul. "Now is the judgement of this world: now shall the prince of this world be cast out" (John 12:31). "Now" signifies the time when Jesus goes to the cross and surrenders himself totally to the will and glory of God. In the lowliness of the cross he will be exalted, by his subjection to death he will rise to life. "Now . . . the prince of this world cometh" (John 14:30), and through Judas, the Jews and Pilate, overpowers Jesus, hoping to destroy him through having him tried by the world; but he only condemns himself (John 16:11), and is defeated, while Jesus, whom he hoped to accuse and condemn, ascends to the Father.

According to St. Paul "the princes of this world" have crucified "the Lord of glory". If they "had but known the

[38] This is the reason for the practice of the sign of the cross: to exorcise and turn away the devil, a practice which goes back to the earliest times of Christianity. See the learned essay of E. Dinkler, "Jesu Wort vom Kreuztragen" in *Neutestamentliche Studien für R. Bultmann* (2nd ed., 1957), pp. 110–29.

wisdom of God", they would never have crucified the "Lord of glory" (1 Cor. 2:8), for the wisdom of God ordained their death in the death of Jesus, and his death destroyed them totally. But they did not know him; although they knew about him, they did not recognize him. They feared him, in the same way as St. James tells us (2:19) the demons tremble before God. For all self-willed beings are at heart afraid of God. But because of the pride of their nature they did not yield to this fear, ánd so they did not humble themselves before Jesus of Nazareth. In all his craftiness the devil is fundamentally foolish, which is no contradiction of his craftiness – and the demons did not realize that obedient love is not only stronger than death, even and precisely when it suffers death, as it always will, but also in the very act of dying destroys all being that lives apart from God. This they learn through Jesus Christ whom they crucified, whom God raised from the dead "setting him on his right hand in the heavenly places. Above all principality, and power, and virtue, and domin-ion, and every name . . ." (Eph. 1:21), and, "despoiling the principalities and powers, he hath exposed them confi-dently in open show, triumphing over them" on the cross (Col. 2:15).[39]

Of course, for the time being, the triumph of the crucified, risen and glorified Jesus Christ over the principalities is hidden, and in that sense it is not yet final as far as the world is con-cerned. The overthrow of the principalities and of their master, and the breaking of their power will be revealed, finally for mankind at the Second Coming of Jesus Christ, at his appear-

[39] See also Phil. 2:5–11; 1 Peter 3:22.

ance in majesty at the end of time. Eternal punishment will then be dealt out to them.[40]

Until that moment of ultimate decision, weakened as they are by the death and resurrection of Jesus Christ, the powers have no future but their approaching ruin. Until then they are "the princes of this world that come to naught (οἱ καταργούμενοι)", as St. Paul calls them in 1 Cor. 2:6; they shall come to "everlasting fire which was prepared for the devil and his angels" (Matt. 25:41).

But until then they will also be excluded from the place where Jesus Christ is. The place before God's throne is taken by Jesus Christ who died and rose again, "who also maketh intercession for us" (Rom. 8:34),[41] for he died and rose for us; while the accuser and his accusation are thrust down from his place (Apoc. 12:10). This implies that, until that moment, the principalities can always be driven from the place which Jesus Christ occupies on this earth as well, from the "body of Christ", which is the Church; and they have no choice but to yield.

It is thus not to be supposed that the power of the principalities has been broken only provisionally by Jesus Christ, and that this will not be made manifest until his Second Coming, so that as far as the present time is concerned, nothing has actually changed. It is not to be thought that, while the present time is subject to the terror and pressure of the principalities, Christians, like the Jews, can only hope for their annihilation in the messianic future. There has been a change, and it is decisive. Victory has been gained, and the principalities have been con-

[40] See also Matt. 25:41; 1 Cor. 15:24; Apoc. 20:10.
[41] See also Heb. 7:25; 9:24.

quered. The victory has been gained by God in Jesus Christ for our sake. During this time, however, we must indeed be on the side of Jesus Christ and continue his victory. We must even now live from this victory in him who has defeated the principalities.

The conquest of the principalities by Jesus Christ has, indeed, wrought a fundamental change in the state of the world. We said with the New Testament that now the future of the principalities is but the fulfillment of the sentence which was passed upon them by the cross and resurrection of Christ. They have no other expectation than the final breaking of their power and their eternal damnation. The New Testament tells us that this can already be seen in their present nature and activity. It can be recognized in the first place in the growing frenzy of their nature in the world and in the concentration of their gradual attack on the Church. It can also be inferred, in that there is one place in this world where they can never settle, but from which they will always be expelled; this place has been occupied and is held by Jesus Christ through his victory over the principalities; in it he continues until the end of time his conquest of these powers. This place is the Church on earth.

It is not by accident that the spirit of evil is growing more frenzied, for Jesus has broken its power, and this realization inspires panic. St. Matthew (8:28) tells us that as soon as the demons saw Jesus they were filled with dread of their imminent downfall: "And when he was come on the other side of the water, into the country of the Gerasenes, there met him two that were possessed with devils, coming out of the sepulchres, exceeding fierce, so that none could pass by that way. And, behold, they cried out saying: 'What have we to do with thee, Jesus Son of God? Art thou come hither to torment us before the time?'" The time of which they speak is the time of judgement, which has come upon them with Christ's cross and resurrection; and ever since they are filled with anguish.

The effect of Christ's cross and resurrection is summed up in the hymn which John, the seer of the Apocalypse, heard a "loud voice in heaven" sing: "Therefore, rejoice, O heavens, and you that dwell therein. Woe to the earth and to the sea, because the devil is come down unto you, having great wrath, knowing that he hath but a short time." We may say in the sense of the Apocalypse that the devil is left only with time and no longer with eternity (Apoc. 12:10). And his very finiteness fills him with fear of his eternal damnation. He does not submit to this despair, for in his fear, too, he remains his own master, but it spills over in "rage", and this rage curtails even more the time which is left to him. The spirit of raging haste now breaks forth from his fear, and turns into the spirit of the time which is still left to him. Time, interpreted by fear, hastens ever since Christ was born. Suddenly it becomes important to win time, to advance in and with time, to overtake what evaporates ever more swiftly. The atmosphere of human history is increasingly filled with the fear of time. Characteristic of it is man's forgetting of his transient status and his dreams of his own eternity. Each man absorbs this fear of time with which the dominating spirit has filled the world, and passes it on in his thoughts, deeds and attitude. Men are aware of lost time, and their attempts seemingly to recapture it preoccupy them.[42] A peculiar fea-

---

[42] For example, in the apparent recapturing of the nature of time in literary form, as in the work of Proust.

ture of human history since Christ is that frenzy which springs from the fear of time due to men's unwillingness to recognize that time has passed. That rage-laden atmosphere is discharged in those immense and increasing catastrophes of history. This is made clear in the New Testament in answer to those who complain that the world has not become "better" in the time of the Church. Not only does the awe-inspiring Apocalypse show this, but also the Apocalyptic discourse of our Lord in the Synoptic Gospels, the Testament of Jesus Christ, which should be called the prologue to his Covenant. There we see that the final situation of mankind is considered to be so oppressive, that God's ultimate curtailment of time is regarded as mankind's very opportunity to survive in God's presence (Mark 13:19 et seq.).

This rage which fills the spirit of self-will and with which he fills the world, is naturally always directed against him who has and grants time, against God. It is also directed against God's new creation, the Church which, through hope, already shares in God's time. For in the wisdom of the Redeemer and through the Church the wisdom of the Creator which is everlasting has been manifested to the world. In the Church it is now opposed to all principalities as eternal refuge for all men whom the spirit of time has made afraid.[43] For it is together with Christ that the members of this Church have been raised and exalted from the dead into the eternity of grace.

That is also the reason for the violent attacks upon "the child" and "the woman and her seed" (Apoc. 12:4, 13 et seq.).

---

[43] See Eph. 2:5 et seq. and 3:10. On these see H. Schlier, *Der Brief an die Epheser* (1957), pp. 112 et seq., and 156 et seq.

50

The Apocalypse shows us that the spirit which inspires this anxiety about time goes to fantastic lengths in these attacks, whether they are overt or surreptitious. He thereby reveals his frenzied despair at the knowledge that his end is near. Because he realizes that the eternal power of Jesus Christ is already present in the Church, she becomes his principal target, the last stronghold which he wants to conquer either openly or by stealth, from outside or from within.

On a broad view, human history appears as a great struggle between the principalities and the Church; this collision of the principalities and the "lasting city" results in the downfall of the spirits. It is only on rare occasions that this struggle is played out openly; but it is always present. It is not just a romantic dream of the Church over-estimating herself. It is already recognized in the New Testament at the very beginning and source of the Church.

As we have seen, the principalities were never far from Jesus during his life on earth.[44] The Wicked One even causes Peter to discourage Jesus from undergoing his passion and incites Judas to betray him.[45] His legions have crucified the Lord. He now also steals the word from the hearts of men, and sows tares among the wheat. He begets "children of the wicked one".[46] The "god of this world" blinds men to the light which shines from the Gospel.[47] In a particular case he prevents the apostle from visiting his communities.[48] And it is he who

[44] Luke 22:28; see 4:1 et seq., and parallel passage; 22:31 et seq.
[45] Mark 8:32 et seq.; Luke 22:3; John 6:70; 13:12.
[46] Mark 4:15 and parallel passages; Mark 13:25; 13:37 et seq.
[47] 2 Cor. 4:4.
[48] Rom. 1:13; 15:22; 1 Thess. 2:18.

51

brings sufferings upon Christians in order to cause them to apostatize.[49] As the Christians when they were still pagans were drawn into the orbit of idols, so even now they are in danger of falling under the power of the gods and demons.[50]

Heresy grows alongside the Church like a twin brother; and is filled with the spirit of perversion and pride. In the self-willed interpretation of the apostolic message by the Gnostics and other heretics is reflected its infiltration, penetrated by the intellectual power of Satan.[51]

But enough of this "struggle", these "wars" and "assaults", and "burning arrows" of the spirit.[52] The New Testament makes it clear that the onslaught of the principalities, while affecting creation generally, has now as its supreme objective Jesus Christ and his Church. The Church is the scene of the triumph of the majesty of Jesus, and in it even now – though in an obscure and symbolic fashion – justice and truth rise up in and through her members, not deriving from pride and not reflecting self-seeking. And the Church is also the realm in and through which the principalities are defeated time and again by Jesus Christ, and where their final ruin is foreshadowed.

[49] Apoc. 2:10.   [50] 1 Cor. 12:2; Apoc. 9:20.
[51] See Rom. 15:20; 2 Cor. 11:1 et seq.; Col. 2:18; 1 Tim. 4:1; 2 Tim. 2:26; 1 John 4:1 et seq.
[52] See Eph. 6:11 et seq., 16; Apoc. 12:17; 13:7.

III

THE CHRISTIAN AND THE PRINCIPALITIES

FINALLY we wish to consider the manner and the sense in which, according to the New Testament, the principalities can be exorcized and expelled through Christ and Christians in the Church. How is the eschatological victory of Jesus Christ on the cross continued in the Church and through the Church?

We have pointed out already that the power of the principalities has been broken through the death and resurrection of Jesus Christ. According to the New Testament, Christians have already been accepted into Jesus Christ, his death and resurrection, and into his victory over the principalities, when they became Christians through Baptism. St. Paul tells the Romans: "Know you not that all we who are baptized in Christ Jesus are baptized in his death? For we are buried together with him by Baptism into death: that, as Christ is risen from the dead by the glory of the Father, so we also may walk in newness of life" (6:3 et seq.). Thus the life of each single Christian has once already been incorporated into the events of Christ's life and has entered upon a new course of justice, truth, and sanctity, through the power of the Holy Ghost to whom these are owing. But Baptism and regeneration have had another effect on the baptized person, which is often overlooked. Because he came from Adam, man was subject to the principalities and powers and to the wicked spirit.

By Baptism, God has released him from this subjection.

Baptism transfers the life of the Christian into a dimension that is still within the grasp of the principalities, exposed to their attacks, indeed, more so than ever: but through the power of the Holy Ghost, Christians are enabled to ward off these assaults, and triumph over the demons, provided they remain in this new dimension of faith. This is the meaning of the prayer of thanksgiving which St. Paul quotes in Col. 1:12 et seq.: "Giving thanks to God the Father, who hath made us worthy to be partakers of the lot of the saints in light: who hath delivered us from the power of darkness, and hath translated us into the kingdom of the Son of his love." The same idea recurs in Eph. 2:5 et seq.: God, "even when we were dead in sins, hath quickened us together in Christ – by whose grace you are saved – and hath raised us up together and hath made us sit together in the heavenly places, that he might shew in the ages to come the abundant riches of his grace, in his bounty towards us in Christ Jesus." This passage refers to Baptism, by which we are not yet removed from the sphere where the demons operate, for the principalities have their abode in the "heavens" of this world and of men; but by Baptism we can be safe in Jesus Christ in this place of perils, and thereby protected in obedience.

Baptism exposes, as it were, the conditions of our existence, it places us in an exposed situation. But it is a situation that is open towards God. We are placed there as men who "in Jesus Christ" have access to God. It is precisely this access which the principalities seek to prevent. Thus they try to keep men away from Baptism, and to prevent those who have been baptized from abiding in Jesus Christ. What matters is for the baptized to hold firmly to the decision which tore them from subjection to the principalities and made them Christians.[53]

According to the New Testament, however, this happens primarily in faith. The decision to turn to God is made in faith, and it is in faith that we persevere in this decision. Faith is

[53] This is expressed neatly and correctly in a somewhat uncouth style in the Epistle of Barnabas, 16:6–10: "Let us now enquire whether there is a temple of God. There is a temple in the place where he himself promised to build and prepare one . . . I find . . . that there really is a temple of God. Learn how it shall be built in the name of the Lord. Before we came to believe in God, the abode of our heart was weak and liable to decay, just like a temple made with hands; for it was full of idolatry and a dwelling place of demons, since we did what was opposed to God. 'But it shall be built in the name of the Lord'. Note well how the temple shall be built gloriously. How? Learn: by receiving forgiveness of sin and placing our hope in his name, we become new and are re-created from the beginning. God then really dwells in us in our abode. In what manner? We are led into the indestructible temple by the word of his faith, by the call of his promise, by the wisdom of his instructions, by the precepts of his teaching, by him himself speaking in us prophetically and dwelling in us who were the slaves of death, and opening the door of the temple (namely, the mouth) and converting us. For if anyone wishes to be saved, he does not look to men, but to him who dwells and speaks within him; he is amazed, because never before did he hear the words of him who speaks from the mouth of man, and he never had the desire to hear them. That is the spiritual temple which is built in the Lord."

Neither in the New Testament, nor in the first echo of the apostles' preaching to be found in the Apostolic Fathers, is it held that, through Baptism, man is withdrawn once for all from the principalities. They rather teach that Baptism, as the source and origin of a new life, frees man's beginnings from their domination, and leaves him free to persevere in faith. To this extent we may agree with the censure which R. Schnackenburg (in *Das Heilsgeschehen bei der Taufe nach dem Apostel Paulus* [1950], p. 8, note 21) passes upon the "material-magical inter-

basically man's turning to the God of Jesus Christ in answer to his call. This involves turning away from idols, and, therefore, also from self-will. St. Paul reminds the Christians of Thessalonica "how you turned to God from idols to serve the living and true God" (1 Thess. 1:9). This faith reveals that "an idol is nothing in the world, and there is no God but one. For although there be that are called gods, either in heaven or on earth (for there be gods many and lords many), yet to us there is but one God, the Father, of whom are all things, and we unto him: and one Lord Jesus Christ, by whom are all things, and we by him" (1 Cor. 8:4–6). This faith holds firmly that the gods and lords, the principalities and powers, are really nothing, even when they dominate mankind and the world with great power, indeed with the power of death.

The Christian knows in faith the feebleness of all the claims by which they try to drive mankind under the fatal influence of a self-powered, self-reliant, and self-seeking life of pride. "If then you be dead with Christ from the elements of this world" – which Baptism has achieved – "why do you yet decree as though living in the world?" (Col. 2:20).[54] Faith knows the transient character of the claims which the "elements" advance,

pretation" of W. Heitmueller (in *Im Namen Jesu* [1903], p. 280, cf. pp. 307 et seq.; and in *Taufe und Abendmahl im Urchristentum* [1911], p. 9), and of R. Bultmann, who is much more cautious, in *Neutestamentliche Theologie* (2nd ed., 1954), p. 137 (126). But this should not blind us to the ontological significance of Baptism. Without it much of the unfolding baptismal liturgy of early Christianity would be unintelligible, and Baptism would lose an essential element which this liturgy has opened up.

[54] It is possible to illustrate how mankind – even Christians – is ruled by such decrees today. We proudly speak of our age as the "atomic age".

because it knows the transience of the principalities which inspire these claims. Faith knows that Christ has overcome the principalities on the cross; because of this knowledge, and in so far as it surrenders unconditionally to Christ, faith recognizes the weakness of the principalities and of their claims. This faith is built upon Christ's victory; in it man is set above all principalities.

This implies that faith is inseparable from obedience. The world spirit which dominates the pagan atmosphere is described in Eph. 2:2 as "the spirit that now worketh on the children of unbelief". This unbelief begins and ends with the rejection of the message of Jesus Christ.[55] When men fall away from the Gospel, they again become followers and subjects of this spirit.[56] One of the principal effects of Christ's message, in whatever shape or form it appears, is to reveal clearly and unerringly the state in which the domination of the principalities places men, then inviting men to the triumph of Christ over these principalities in his cross and resurrection. It then drags these principalities from their hiding places, tears away their mask of exaggerated importance or pretended harmlessness, and reveals them stripped of their pretences in their undisguised reality.

For the first time in human history, man has named "an epoch of human existence after the provision of a force of nature". This has been examined in detail from a philosophical standpoint by M. Heidegger, in Der Satz vom Grund (1957), pp. 199 et seq. From a theological point of view, this can only be regarded as the subjection of mankind to the claims of the powers of the elements which prevail over man because he himself has enabled them to do so.

[55] See John 3:36; Acts 14:2; 19:9; Rom. 2:18; 11:30 et seq.; 15:31; Eph. 5:6; Heb. 3:18; 4:6,11; 11, 31; 1 Peter 2:7 et seq.; 3:1; 20; 4:17.

[56] 1 Tim. 5:15; see also 2 Thess. 2:9–12.

But if a man hears and accepts Christ's message with faith and abides in it, he penetrates the fog of illusions with which the principalities shroud the world and human existence. He will recognize at their true value the threats and temptations which accompany existence as presented by them to man, and so he breaks free from what in 1 Tim. 3:7 is aptly described as "the snare of the devil": for the Gospel has taught him that Christ has left the devil only whatever power unbelief allows him.

Faith, as obedience to the message of Christ in the Church, must be expressed in the works of faith. The ever-new resolve of faith must become a resolute faith. To take but one example, such resolve is suggested by "putting on the armour of God", as St. Paul says in Eph. 6:10 et seq.: "Finally, brethren, be strengthened in the Lord and in the might of his power. Put you on the armour of God, that you may be able to stand against the deceits of the devil. For our wrestling is not against flesh and blood; but against principalities and powers, against the rulers of the world of this darkness, against the spirits of wickedness in the high places. Therefore take unto you the armour of God, that you may be able to resist in the evil day and to stand in all things perfect. Stand, therefore, having your loins girt about with truth, and having on the breastplate of justice: and your feet shod with the preparation of the gospel of peace. In all things taking the shield of faith, wherewith you may be able to extinguish all the fiery darts of the most wicked one. And take unto you the helmet of salvation and the sword of the spirit (which is the word of God), by all prayer and supplication praying."

In St. Paul's threefold call upon Christians to put on the

armour of God, we are exhorted not only to trust in these virtues, but to clothe ourselves with truth, justice, peace, hope and the word of God. These are all supported by faith, which is the shield to repel the fiery darts of the Wicked One, and also to smother and quench their flame.

The struggle against the evil principalities can consist in man's surrender of himself to truth. This means not to flinch from the reality of things as revealed by the Gospels, but to face and to surrender to it by an act of informed judgement. When the Christian does this, he manifests reality in himself, and through him it appears in the world, freed now from the sheen of self-will which the principalities impart to it.

To proclaim the Gospel of peace is another expression of the struggle against the powers of evil. The Christian should be ready in faith to carry out the message of peace in word and deed. Whether he will thereby attain exterior peace for himself is doubtful, no less so whether he will succeed in creating peace around him. This does not depend on him alone. But to be ready for peace means choosing peace on all occasions, in the midst of a world full of strife, in which the powers have established discord as their very principle. But this choice can only be made in the belief that peace has already come and has been established in him of whom it is said: "He is our peace", and "coming he preached peace".[57] But when this choice is made, there is the chance that in at least one place on earth evil's commitment to discord may be dissolved and peace may arise, which may spread from peace of human hearts to peace among nations.

[57] See Eph. 2:14 et seq., 17 et seq.

These examples show that the struggle against the wicked powers to which the apostle calls Christians is not the kind of struggle in which men usually engage. To begin with, it is not waged only, nor even mainly, with weapons which we draw from our vital or moral resources. Secondly, the opponent is not only, nor primarily, an outsider; it is not even an enemy separate from ourselves. Finally, we cannot expect an outward victory in this fight.

The struggle against the principalities is always a movement of faith. Indeed it cannot be waged otherwise than through a struggle against oneself. For these enemies, the principalities, always have an ally within us, the sin derived from Adam, which, even in those who have received Baptism, is always manifest as a constant tendency towards the self and away from God and from our neighbour whom God has sent to us, and to whom he has sent us. The ally of the principalities within me is my false love of self and my turning away from God and from my neighbour to which, in the sins of injustice and self-righteousness, I repeatedly succumb.

It is shown in Eph. 2:1 et seq., that when a man surrenders to his pride, his self-willed independence, and his "desire", he will live according to the rule of the proud spirit which controls everything by dominating the "air". We may also infer the converse from this passage, that when a man gives in to his selfish desires, he thereby falls under the influence of that world which is under the seductive or menacing power of the dominating spirit. And, therefore by sin, self-righteousness and injustice, we recognize in practice the apparently unbroken authority of the principalities. When an individual sins, he accepts in effect the interpretation which the principalities present, of himself and of themselves, and he aids the nature of the evil powers.

That is why St. Paul can say: "Let not the sun go down upon your anger. Give not place to the devil" (Eph. 4:26 et seq.). This may appear exaggerated, for what has a man's anger to do with the devil? When a man gives way to anger he makes a place within himself for the devil, and he gives the devil and his ruinous power a foothold in the world. Through his anger the man helps, as it were, to intensify the atmosphere of evil. Again, 1 Tim. 3:6 shows that through conceit a man may fall under the judgement of the devil and his ignominious snare. And in 2 Cor. 2:10 et seq. the apostle remarks that Satan outwits men when they are unforgiving. The whole matter is summed up in 1 John 3:8: "He that committeth sin is of the devil: for the devil sinneth from the beginning."

These statements are not to be understood as expressions of an exaggerated moralism which has elevated a simple moral rule to a law of religion and which are best discarded altogether. St. Paul's words rather indicate the actual place of sin, its scope and the depth of its effects. They also teach something that is most important in the present context, that the struggle against the principalities fundamentally begins with and in myself. If I am to resist and drive out the devil and not merely to strengthen his power, this struggle can only be waged, by my denying myself to him and choosing and abiding in truth, justice, peace, and hope. When the struggle against the principalities is thus fought by giving myself up in faith to justice and serving it, and, as St. Paul says, by presenting my "members" as "instruments of justice" (cf. Rom. 6:13), the

61

devil will be expelled, his sham righteousness exposed. At the same time, the righteousness of Christ will be displayed, and thereby the right order of creation made clear, enduring and always at our service in spite of the mutilations which it suffers.

The New Testament repeatedly declares that this struggle against the principalities is an infinitely hard struggle because it is also a fight against sin. If justice, truth, peace and salvation generally, are to wrestle successfully with injustice, falsehood, unrest and havoc – which, since Adam have determined the course of the world because of the alliance between the principalities and sin – this will come about only through sacrifices, and finally through the sacrifice for which the sacrifice of Christ was the model. In every little sacrifice by which I yield to the justice and truth which have been manifested again in Christ, I imitate that model.

The enemy is powerless against this sacrifice, for he has no foothold or support in it for his self-willed nature. He is passed over in this sacrifice as though he no longer existed, and indeed he is no more for the man who accepts sacrifice for the sake of God. And that is why, though we can seldom see it, time curtailed by Satan's anxious frenzy draws nourishment from the blood of martyrs and the sacrifice of saints. In the eyes of this world they are evidently defeated; but this is their victory. Those innumerable faithful ones of various degrees, many of whose very names are unknown, create, both for themselves and for other men new hearts, spaces, times and spheres where the power of the devil is no more, and where is the beginning of God's kingdom of justice, truth, peace and joy in the Holy Ghost. It is only occasionally and temporarily that their sacrifice produces such enclaves on earth. But they are signs of what will be all-embracing and final.[58]

This victory over the principalities that begins in faith, progress through good works, and reaches its consummation in suffering with Christ, is supported according to the New Testament by prayer. St. Matthew (17:19 et seq.), relates that on one occasion the disciples of Jesus were unable to drive out a demon because they had not the faith which moves mountains; when Jesus himself drove out the demon, they came to him secretly and asked: "Why could not we cast him out?" Jesus answered: "This kind is not cast out but by prayer and fasting"

[58] It is not out of place to clarify in this context the way in which the New Testament uses the terms "victory" and "to overcome". The terms appear only in the Johannine writings and they are used in three ways, which really express one truth.

1. At the Last Supper Jesus speaks of his victory, in John 16:33: "In the world you shall have distress. But have confidence. I have overcome the world" (ἐγὼ νενίκηκα τὸν κόσμον). He has triumphed over what the prince of this world presents as world of death and darkness, and, therefore, also of "distress" (θλῖψις). And the reference is to the victory which Jesus gained on the cross in what appeared to the world as an utter defeat; for on the cross, on his way to his Father, he persevered in his love for the world. 2. There is, however, reference also to the victory of the faith and of the faithful, for example in 1 John 5:4: "And this is the victory which overcometh the world: our faith"; cf. also 2:13; 4:4; and Apoc. 2:26. Faith here is concrete faith in Jesus as Son of God. The man who has this faith wins perfectly the victory of faith which believes in the victory won by Jesus. He is victorious in so far as in faith he no longer believes in the world, nor consequently in the way in which the principalities interpret the world; he, therefore, draws life again from God, and from this new life he complies "in love" with all God's instructions (the "commandments"). "Whatsoever is born of God overcometh the world" (1 John 5:4). 3. The verb "to overcome" is

(Mark 9:28 et seq.). It is manifest that the early Christian community realized the implications of this statement.

Our prayer – "through Jesus Christ our Lord" – must be determined[59] and unwearying; man must turn only to the giver of all power: he must be ready for God's gift. Nothing except such prayer can break through the impenetrable sphere of the spell which the spirit of pride lays upon the world and men.[60] That is why our Lord himself concluded the Our Father with the petition: "Deliver us from evil" (Matt. 6:13), and why on behalf of his disciples he asks God "that thou shouldst keep them from evil" (John 17:15). That was in St.

applied eminently to those who have overcome the devil, "the accuser of our brethren", by giving testimony with their lives to him who has overcome, the "lion" who is also "the lamb" (Apoc. 5:5), who shall overcome (Apoc. 17:14). "And they overcame him by the blood of the lamb and by the word of the testimony: and they loved not their lives unto death" (Apoc. 12:11). Their victory is based on the victory of Christ, in so far as they take Christ's victory and repeat it as testimony in their own victory. Martyrdom, as testimony to Christ, continues fully and completely the victory by which Christ broke the power of the principalities of death.

[59] That is the significance of the variant reading in Mark 9:28: προσ-ευχῇ καὶ νηστείᾳ 𝔓45(?) ACDW ΘλφΚ vg syᶜ ᵖᵉ sa, which probably represents the original text.

[60] See E. Peterson, *Marginalien zur Theologie* (1956), pp. 98 et seq.: "St. Paul teaches that our struggle is not against flesh and blood, but against the rulers of this world of darkness, against the spirits of wickedness in the high places, against the prince who has power over the air. . . . To fight against flesh and blood, against Marx and Hegel, is nothing compared to that atheism which we breathe in with the air. It is this atheism of the prince of this world which we breathe in with the air that threatens to smother us; it prevents our prayer from rising up to heaven; we lose what the ancients called Parrhesia, the ability to pray. . . ."

Paul's mind when he urged the Church to pray unceasingly as a part of the struggle against the principalities (Eph. 6:18).

Finally in this context we ought to consider two injunctions of the apostles. The first is in 1 Peter 5:8: "Be sober and watch: because your adversary the devil, as a roaring lion, goeth about seeking whom he may devour. Whom resist ye, strong in faith."

The first injunction is "Be sober and watch". Sobriety[61] here means freedom from illusions. Such sobriety is aware of the devil and his principalities and of the state of temptation and suffering created by him in this world; but this sobriety is not intimidated by the devil nor by the menace of the world under his domination.[62] Watchfulness springs from this fearless knowledge of the reality of these principalities and their effectiveness; it guards against the snares of this spirit; it is calmly aware of what is really happening in this world. Watchfulness here means the clear awareness of the basic ambiguity with which his atmosphere, the air of self-glorification, envelops all things and events. Watchfulness also knows of the infinite disguises in which he approaches men, and of the reluctance of the human will to see through him.

Linked with sobriety and watchfulness is a second injunction:

---

[61] νήφω (νηφάλιος) is one of those unexpected descriptions of Christian existence which calls for a full theological investigation. See the brief exposition of Bauernfeind ThWB 935–940. The same applies to γρηγορεῖν which is not treated at all in ThWB.

[62] See *Pastor Hermae, mand.* XII, 4, 6: "Fear not the devil, for he has no power over you"; 4, 7: "The devil injects only fear, but his fear is powerless"; 5, 2: "The devil cannot crush the servants of God who hope in God with their whole heart. The devil can wrestle with them, but he cannot throw them." See also 6, 1.

"Try the spirits" (1 John 4:1). We are constantly to awaken, to practise, and to guard the *charisma* of discernment of spirits (1 Cor. 14:1). The discerning of spirits is a gift of the Holy Ghost, and St. Paul teaches that we should be "zealous" for such gifts (1 Cor. 14:1). Frequently there is only a thin dividing line between good and bad spirits, and it is only a clear and sharp insight which God grants us that can tell the difference, and dispel the mist which the evil spirit deliberately creates. Where this gift is lacking, there is a danger that we may suspect the dark influence of the devil to be at work everywhere, so that we may never recognize him when he is really there; or we may minimize his presence and fail to see him even when he is in our midst.

Man who, by Baptism, has already been delivered from the principalities, is thus called to resist them in the name of Jesus Christ who has overcome them.[63] His resistance must be based on faith, loyalty, good works, prayer, sober vigilance, and the charismatic discernment of spirits. Though their power is broken, the principalities dominate this world, and it is only when man obeys the call, that the victory which Christ gained over them on the cross is made visible and their perdition is foreshadowed.

We must also remember what Jesus told the seventy disciples when they returned to him in delight because even demons were subject to them in his name. He told them that Satan had fallen from heaven like lightning, and that he had given to his disciples authority over all the powers of Satan and that nothing could harm them. But he continues: "But yet rejoice not in

[63] See also Jas. 4:7 et seq.

this, that spirits are subject to you: but rejoice in this, that your names are written in heaven" (Luke 10:17-20). And this is echoed by Ignatius, the Bishop of Antioch, when he wrote to the Christian communities of Asia Minor shortly before his martyrdom: "Even I who in my chains know the things of heaven, the places of the angels, the hosts of the powers, visible and invisible, am not yet a disciple. For much is yet needed so that God may not be missed" (Trall. 5:2).

In conclusion we shall list as propositions the points which have been established.

1. The manifold principalities which unfold the one satanic power are encountered as a kind of personal and powerful being.

2. These principalities exercise their being by taking possession of the world as a whole, and of individual men, the elements, political and social institutions, historical conditions and circumstances, spiritual and religious trends. Above all, their possession is exercised mainly through the "atmosphere", which is the immediate site of their power.

3. They take possession of the world and of men in such a way that they let these appear in their spirit. Withdrawing and concealing themselves, they reveal themselves through the world and existence, of which they have taken possession, and which they transcend in themselves.

4. They interpret the world and existence unto death, as temptation and falsehood. Death, sin and falsehood mark the inmost tendency of their nature, and, therefore, its fruit. These are the effects of their inmost nature, in which they act against their origin: in self-aggrandizement and independent pride, in which they and their present nature struggle against their original creatureliness.

5. These principalities have been overcome by God in Jesus Christ on the cross and in the resurrection and exaltation of Jesus. Their power has thereby been broken, in so far as their proud autonomy has been drawn into the love of the obedient Son of God which embraces even them, and has been undone in his death.

6. Their power has been broken on the cross and in the resurrection. Like everything else which happened there, this will be finally and completely revealed in the Second Coming of Christ Triumphant. Their defeat will then be shown to be eternal rejection. Until then, mankind and the world must suffer the ever-increasing attacks of the principalities which know that they have been judged and, therefore, increase their anxious frenzy. Having no other future than eternal damnation, the principalities concentrate their attack on those who have an eternal future, namely, the Church and her members.

7. The members of the Church who have already been delivered from the principalities in Baptism in Jesus Christ, must resist them the more strongly. Their aim must be to defeat the principalities in faith and loyalty, in works of justice and truth, in unceasing prayer, sober and vigilant, with the gift of the discernment of spirits. They must also endeavour through sacrifice to create in the Church a place free from their domination, as a sign of the new heavens and the new earth which are to come.

ANTICHRIST

On the thirteenth chapter of the Apocalypse of St. John

IT is well known that the coming of Antichrist is often mentioned in the New Testament. Before the nature of Antichrist can be determined in general, these passages have to be interpreted individually. For this purpose the thirteenth chapter of St. John's Apocalypse is one of the most interesting and fruitful sources.[1]

The context of this chapter is the "revelation of Jesus Christ". It occurs at the point where the history of the world is unrolled in the light of God's decree which takes place in Jesus Christ.

In chapter 1:9–20, the seer records "the things which he has seen" (1:19), namely the appearance of the Lord Triumphant, "one like to the Son of man". The next two chapters describe "the things which are". They tell about the Church of Asia Minor, whose seven communities represent the new era of the Church, oppressed by the guile and power of Satan, but guided and consoled by the word of her Lord.

This is followed by chapters 4 to 20, which with chapter 22 show "the things which must be done hereafter", namely the appearance of Jesus Christ in judgement at the end of the world. This third main section of the Apocalypse reveals the events

[1] In general I have not given references for individual points. The reader is referred to the current commentaries, particularly those of Bousset, Charles, Lohmeyer, and Hadorn.

which shall accompany the coming of the Lord in judgement "as a thief" (3:3).

In chapter 4, the author lets us see in all his glory the majesty of him who sits in the throne and reigns for ever. Then the Lamb appears. He alone can open the book of destiny in which the history of the world is contained, because he has conquered. The history which is hidden is revealed to him, for he has endured it; it tells how judgement is passed on the universe before the end of time.[2]

The seals are then opened after the other, and this history is revealed stage by stage; like an army of destructive powers and forces the future sweeps over the horizon. While this is going on, the blood which the martyrs have shed calls for the day of fulfillment that is long in coming. The great day of "wrath" is close at hand, as the fabric of the world collapses and inspires such terror that death seems a refuge from it. At this point there is the consoling vision of the full number of those who are sealed in the Church Triumphant, the Israel of all nations, "who are come out of great tribulation" (chapter 7). This is all the more consoling in view of the following new

[2] It is the history which is already world-judgement, but not in the sense as though history itself could judge and decide. It can no more do that than it can correct God's decrees: cf. Rom. 9:6: "Not as though the word of God has miscarried." The claim of history to pass judgement is contradicted by Jas. 2:13: "Mercy exalteth itself above judgement." There is, however, a sense in which world history is judgement on the world, for the wrath of God makes itself felt in history and produces the terror of "the day of wrath and revelation of the just judgement of God" (Rom. 2:5). St. Paul also teaches that this is the state of the universe: "The wrath of God is revealed from heaven against all ungodliness and injustice of those men that detain the truth of God in injustice" (Rom. 1:18).

70

vision of the breaking of the last seal and the uncovering of the foundation of history, which is the theme of this passage; step by step new destruction is wrought upon the conditions of life, and cruel havoc is worked upon the earth and among its inhabitants by the released demoniacal powers (chapters 8 and 9).

But only partly are "the things which must be done hereafter" thereby revealed, only the surface of the events in which there is a foreshadowing of the Final Judgement at Christ's coming. These catastrophes are merely the symptoms of the judgement to come. Hidden as yet is the really historical side of the crisis, namely the judgement which takes place upon the human element in the universe. Hidden as yet also are the conditions for the imminent judgement as they have been created in heaven and on earth, also hidden the event of the redemption which has already occurred, and the historical change wrought by this redemption in the universe.

That is why the prophet is ordered in chapter 10 to seal up the message of the seven thunders of judgement (10:3 et seq.). Their events no longer take place in time. History is cut short (cf. Mark 13:20; Matt. 24:22). When the seven trumpets sound, time shall be no more, and the mystery of God shall be fulfilled (10:5–7).

But the seer is also ordered to eat a little open book, a record of events which have already happened, and which can be read about (10:8–10). Then he is to "prophesy again to many nations and peoples and tongues and kings" (10:11). In other words, he is to preface his account of the events concerning the seventh trumpet with a history to be read before he returns to the judgement, but now in its imminent threat for the whole of mankind.

A second part of the prophecy thus begins at 11:1. To some extent it is parallel with chapters 6 to 9. The thread of chapter 9 is resumed in 15:1; but now chapters 11 to 14 provide a foundation for it. Chapters 11 to 20, (22) are in the form of a prophecy which looks upon the universe from the point of view of its end and future in Jesus Christ.

The prophetic perspective of the complete history of Israel is contained in the little book that lies opened in the hand of the mighty angel, and which the seer eats. This history has been reduced to its redemptive fundaments, and emphasizes the eschatological destiny of Israel, which becomes clear in the light of Christ. This is the history of the true Israel which is preserved throughout the whole "two and forty months", the total duration of the eschatological era, while the "court without the temple" and the holy city, the earthly Jerusalem with the Jewish Temple, are destroyed by the Gentiles (11:1–2).[3] It is also the history of the witnesses of Christ (11:3, 8), of the two olive trees and the candlesticks before the sight of God; it is the history of prophecy in the wider sense, including the Law and the Prophets. This history also lasts twelve hundred and sixty days, until the end of time. While the Prophets are to fulfil their commission, they are invincible. But when their testimony is concluded, they will succumb to the beast which comes from the abyss and is now at work, to the delight of "those that dwell upon the earth", tormented as they are by the testimony of these prophets. But then the Prophets hasten to heaven – probably at the resurrection and exaltation of their

[3] As we see from Rom. 11:15, 25 et seq., the salvation of Israel is not an historical but an eschatological event. Therefore, no natural insight can grasp the destiny of the Jews; cf. Rom. 11:25.

Lord – to the terror of their enemies, while the rest acknowledge the glory of God (11:3–13).

The following chapter contains a new vision. There is a double sign in Heaven: the painful[4] birth of the Messias from the heavenly woman, the true Israel, which will then be visible in the Church on earth,[5] and the rescue of the Messias from the mouth of the murderous dragon, the enemy of God (12:1–6). These signs in heaven issue in the victory of the heavenly powers over the forces of Satan, when the devil's power is broken and reduced to finiteness (12:7–9).

This means that for twelve hundred and sixty days, or the "time and times and half a time" ($3^1/_2$ times) for the entire eschatological epoch, heaven stands in the sign of the Church of the desert, the world, persecuted in vain by Satan.

The nature of this persecution is shown in a new vision in chapter 13. There two "beasts" are seen by the seer to rise up. They are Satan's instruments in his "war" against those "who keep the commandments of God and have the testimony of Jesus Christ" (12:17). But what is the prospect of time under

[4] As J. Begel said in *Erklärte Offenbarung Johannis oder vielmehr Jesu Christi,* in the revised edition of W. Hoffmann of 1834, p. 378: "Such travails, pains and cries were the earnest longing, the signs, the ripening expectation of the saints for the kingdom of God. The woman longed and travailed in the Spirit that the kingdom of Christ should appear and she should receive a glance from him as the shepherd and king of all peoples."

[5] It is also heavenly wisdom. In this way we can accept the suggestion which Lohmeyer makes in his commentary. It is reminiscent of the πολυποίκιλος σοφία of Eph. 3:10, which is realized in the Church. The Apocalypse shares something of the background of this idea in Comparative Religion. See H. Schlier, *Christus und die Kirche im Epheserbrief* (1930), pp. 60 et seq.

this heavenly sign? The answer is given in chapter 14. It is the perfected Church of the martyrs in their full number as first fruits destined for God and the Lamb (14:1–5), the echo of the eternal gospel sounding from the zenith across the world (14:6–13), and the appearance in the heavens of "one like to the Son of man" amid the call to judgement of the heavenly messengers (14:14–20).

The sign which dominates the world changes in chapter 15. In the Apocalypse there are only two signs of time differing temporally. Now it is the seven angels with the seven last blows of destiny in which the wrath of God is accomplished. But first there appears once again the vision of the heavenly victors praising God, singing the canticle of Moses and of the Lamb (15:2–4). They soon give way to the other vision in which the seven angels, the cosmic powers, receive from one of the beings, who represent creation, the vials in which the wrath of God is aflame. Now heaven becomes impenetrable for the earth (15:5–8). The voice of the hidden God is heard ordering his wrath to be poured over the earth seven times, and the fabric of the world (chap. 16),[6] to be destroyed.

But the collapse of the cosmic edifice is but the outward sign of the "true and just" judgements of God (16:7). For the hidden God remembers great Babylon (16:19), the mighty city (18:10), which governed the Empire (18:3). To remember Babylon is to recall the judgement passed upon her, which delights all the heavenly voices (17:1 – 19:10).

[6] It is now that the third woe of Apoc. 11:14 comes. It is now that the seventh trumpet sounds over the earth: it had already sounded in heaven before Christ's birth and was answered jubilantly by the heavenly voices (Apoc. 11:15).

Henceforth the seer's vision penetrates even more profoundly and comprehends in clear sequence of events the judgement which increasingly affects the interior of the cosmos. The beast who governs this cosmopolis and his allies are defeated by the Lord himself, and cast into the pool (19:11–21). Satan's power is fettered, and the martyrs and confessors come to life (20:1–6).

The final scene of the eschatological drama is the destruction of Satan, who now gathers his forces for an assault on heaven itself and on the city of God. It concludes with the thrusting down to hell of Satan (20:7–10). Now the universe stands before God's throne and is judged according to its works. Death and its hell are given over to themselves, to the "second death", greater death (20:11–15). But behind the judgement and the death of death is revealed the new heaven and the new earth of God's presence among men (20:1 – 22:5).

This summary of the Apocalypse enables us to place chapter 13 in its context. It forms part of the insertion which, from chapter 10 onwards, surveys the history of time and reveals its eschatological significance.

The general theme of this chapter is the war between the dragon and the individual members of the Church on earth, which as a whole is protected also on earth. The subject of chapter 13 is the world after Christ; it reveals its nature in the light of Christ's coming. It does not deal with events and phenomena beyond the end of time; it concerns the world of finiteness, those "two and forty months" (13:5), which fill past, present and the earthly future of time in which Christ will appear unexpectedly, and which shall last until the natural, political and spiritual foundations of the universe crumble under the blows of judgement.

The Antichrist appearing under the form of two beasts is thus, firstly, a being in time who belongs to the end of history dominated by Christ. Secondly, this "being" makes his appearance not in a particular epoch, though more or less represented in historical phenomena, but with the tendency of identifying himself with concrete historical appearances increasingly until the end. Thirdly, we can infer that Antichrist in this sense is always "contemporary", and therefore in the times after Christ continuously attacks the present. Fourthly, even those mindful of the words of the prophets (1:3; 22:7) will be able to recognize his form in its basic traits only in the perspective of prophecy.

The reader of chapter 13 learns also of the more or less hidden nature of his own history as this is revealed to prophetic insight from the end achieved in Jesus Christ.

What does this chapter of the Apocalypse tell us about the basic traits of Antichrist? The last verse of chapter 12 tells us briefly that Satan "stood upon the sand of the sea" in order to wage war against the seed of the woman. This sea may well be the sea of the world, into which Satan looks, and in which, recognizing himself, he creates his own reflection. The sea is the "abyss" (11:7) of the universe, and is, not inconsistently, at the same time the Western sea where Rome lies, and from which Antichrist comes. This being emerges from the place whence the authority of the Empire extended, as a power emerging from the depths of the world. As it manifests itself on earth and in history it is an "abysmal" phenomenon.

That this being is a reflection of Satan is shown by the similar attributes which it displays as it emerges. Firstly, ten horns with diadems are seen, symbols of royal power and dignity, then the seven heads, signs of total rule in its various exponents who carry names of blasphemy because they have assumed divine marks and appear thus before the world (13:1).

Only after these chief features of the anti-Christian being have been perceived will the form of the Satanic image of Satan itself be visible. "Satan's second in command", as he has been described,[7] has the body of a beast containing those beasts which, according to Daniel 7:1 et seq., represent the kingdoms of this world in their succession. Seen as a whole, it is a shapeless and terrifying earthly power. Only a few characteristic traits are recognizable of this form now spreading across the world. It has the nimbleness of a leopard, the strength of a bear, and the great mouth of a lion. It is not a human, but an animal form. It is the crafty, coarse, and all-devouring Empire,[8] the power of this world governed by bestial instinct, and appearing in bestial form. This is not the "State" as such, the political power which looks after public order; it is the inhuman form of that degenerate political power which is the opposite of public order (13:2).

This reflection of his, which is not a timeless idea but appears on earth in the terrible form of a blindly corrupt empire, Satan has invested with his strength, his throne, and his great power (13:2). For although it is of immense size, this political power is not autonomous, but draws life from Satan, its creator. This "world State" has not only been created by Satan but

---

[7] By Jung-Stilling in *Die Siegsgeschichte der christlichen Religion in einer gemeinnützigen Erklärung der Offenbarung Johannis* (1799), p. 381.

[8] See the description which D. H. Lawrence gives in his commentary on the Apocalypse (1932), p. 269. This work is blinded by anti-Christian feeling, and its scholarship is out of date. Nevertheless it is instructive on many points of detail.

also endowed by him satanically. It is thus a product and an instrument of him whose image it is. It accepts what the Messias refused in the desert (Luke 4:6), and thereby proves that it is essentially opposed to Christ. When it acts, it carries out the decree of Satan, and not the "ordinance of God" (Rom. 13:2). Its thrones are thrones of Satan. The community at Pergamus was an example of people living in the shadow of such a throne (2:13). Instead of serving God, this political power works to serve God's enemy.

Remarkable is the immeasurable power of this phenomenon through constant regeneration. It is no ephemeral apparition but the phenomenon of a whole epoch. The world has the impression that it is eternal (13:3). When one of the heads of the beast, one of the bearers of total power, is mortally wounded, the beast will not die, and the wound will heal again. When one Caesar dies, however serious the blow to the empire, another soon rises in his stead, and the wound is healed. The presence of this political power is never lost. From a natural point of view it is as though the dead were to rise again. It seems as though we could speak of the eternity of such a kingdom, as though the miracle of the everlasting Lamb were here fulfilled in a tangible manner. Seen with the eyes of faith, however, this is precisely where the anti-Christian parody of Christ crucified and risen again shows itself.

The overpowering size of such bestial, earthly power is now recognized also by its impression upon mankind. (13:3-4). The whole earth is astonished before such imperial majesty; it regards the beast as a miracle,[9] just as it later looks upon

---

[9] The Greek verb is: θαυμάζεσθαι.

"Babylon the great" which rides upon the beast (17:8). This must be a work of God, it is said, a miracle "before our eyes". And this miracle compels the earth with one accord to fall prostrate to worship him who is capable of such a miracle of power – the dragon.

The earth loves force, and the secret god, the dragon, is not visible; but the beast can be seen, and it is the visible God who is worshipped. Thus the religion of the beast comes into being. It is clear even from the language in which the beast is worshipped that, it is indeed a religion with which we are dealing, a religious apotheosis of the beast. It is the religious language of the canticle: "Who is like to thee among the strong O God" (Exodus 15:8), and the prayer of Psalm 34:10; "Lord, who is like to thee." In its admiration and fear at the sight of the power of the beast the whole world asks: "Who is like to the beast? And who shall be able to fight with him?" Unconsciously the votaries of this new cult recall the language of their earlier, biblical or other genuine prayers: but their admiration is mixed with fear, and they cannot complete their praise, for the ancient language of genuine worship is not entirely apt for the adoration of this new god. New words and forms are needed for the worship of this fascinating, political power. The new religion is two-faced; it has a disjointed style.

The next four verses (13:5–8) tell us what the beast does on earth, and in what his activity consists. First, he opens his mouth in blasphemies (13:5 et seq.). The mouth is an essential mark of the beast, his mighty speeches, his elevated words. His μεγάλα are almost as numerous as the μεγαλεῖα τοῦ θεοῦ (Acts 2:11). The speech of this god is great and lofty. But the greatness consists essentially of blasphemies. When the beast makes a great utterance, it utters blasphemies. At the end of time this blasphemous mouth will not be silent. It has received the ability to go on in this way for "two and forty months", and it uses its ability: "And he opened his mouth unto blasphemies against God."

Names of blasphemy are on the foreheads of his heads; he is not only capable of blasphemy, but he utters these blasphemies, and turns with blasphemous utterances against the name of God himself, and against his tabernacle, which is the Church, and against her faithful "that dwell in heaven". Blasphemy can, of course, be both direct and indirect. The name of God is blasphemed by mocking and effacing it, but also by falsely ascribing it to the beast. When Caesar is given titles like *Divus Augustus, Dominus ac Deus, Potens Terrarum Dominus, Sacer,* or *Terrarum Gloria;* when men speak of the salvation (*salus,* σωτηρία) which he has brought, and consider his reign a time of salvation and his work as salvation, God's name is injured, and the name of Christ is mocked.[10]

The second activity of the beast is war (13:7) – it is a special kind of war, war against "the saints". This political power acts as well as talks. In so far as it recognizes its enemy, its actions are intelligent. The enemy is not the "kings", for they are its

[10] See Suetonius, *Domitian,* ch. 10: "When he remarried his divorced wife, he did not scruple to say that she had been recalled to his divine throne. Moreover, he was pleased to hear in the amphitheatre the acclamation: 'Hail to our Lord and Our Lady.' . . . When he issued a formal document in the name of his procurators, he showed equal arrogance in beginning thus: 'Our Lord and god orders this to be done.' Henceforth, therefore, it is commanded that he be spoken of by no

allies; they are power from his power (17:11 et seq.). They share his interests in life. They bewail the downfall of the city of the world, the "polis" which the beast dominates (18:9 et seq.). Similarly trade and commerce are not enemies, for the merchants and mariners weep and lament for the fair, rich mistress who bore the empire on her back (18:11, 17 et seq.), and who is now ruined.

The enemies of the beast are the "saints"; there is a kind of metaphysical hereditary enmity between them and the beast. For the beast has taken over this hostility from Satan, its lord. In its fight against the saints, the "great wrath" (12:12) is roused by which Satan is animated ever since he broke loose from God and was thrust down into time. Thus the – in human eyes – strange anti-Christian and anti-Church attitude of the all-pervasive satanic empire expresses but the frustration of evil which, in the knowledge of its imminent end, is filled with envy of those who are not of time but of eternity, the saints, "them that dwell in Heaven". War, that is, the only kind of political activity which this degenerate state-power can exercise in regard to the members of the Church as a whole, always ends on earth with the victory of the political power; the defeat of the saints is assured in advance.

Satan can see no salvation from chaos except the establishment

other name in anyone's writing or speech." See also the inscription from Tegea: "In the sixty-ninth year of the first appearance of the god Hadrian in Greece" (Deissmann, *Licht vom Osten,* 4th ed., p. 319). R. Schütz has assembled numerous examples in: *Die Offenbarung des Johannes und Kaiser Domitian* (1933); see especially pp. 32 et seq. Cf. also Fr. Sauter, *Der römische Kaiserkult bei Martial und Statius* (1934).

of his power; he is afraid of time and ruin, and his secret despair, expressed in such violent rage, drives him beyond his struggle against the saints to unfold his power to such an extent that the entire world falls under his domination (13:7–8). This is the third feature of his activity.

Christ risen said: "All power is given to me on heaven and on earth" (Matt. 28:18). But only faith can appreciate Christ's power on earth, for the beast is master here, of which it is said: "Power was given him over every tribe and people and tongue and nation." It is in the beast that the historical cosmos finds its unity: in him all distinctions are finally abolished. But "freedom", of which the nations naively dream, they will never have. They are subject, either to the kingdom of Satan, or to the kingdom of Christ, and both kingdoms exist in concrete form. Either Christ is the Lord in the body of the Church of which all nations are members, or Satan rules in the degenerate bestial body of his empire consisting of all nations. But in the end there will not be room for the body of Christ, for men rather live under the rule of the beast than under Christ's rule. "And all that dwell upon the earth adored him." They do not reject the beast. This kingdom of blasphemy, persecution and power, is accepted by all except the saints whose names are written in the book of life, those who "from all eternity" know and declare that they are blessed; Christ has chosen them, and at judgement God will call them to life. All others will bend their knees, and finally even their hearts, before the Antichrist. The future will not differ from the past in time; that is why the seer can mix his tenses; the Greek text uses the aorist in 13:4: "They worshipped the beast", and the future tense in 13:8: "They will adore it." The beast claims subjection from the whole world at all times. The worship of the beast is universal both in time and in place.[11]

That is why the seer in 13:9–10 invites his listeners to be attentive, and encourages them: "He that shall lead into captivity shall go into captivity; he that shall kill by the sword must be killed by the sword. Here is the patience and faith of the saints." Christians will recognize the beast and not ignore it; for Christ himself has shown it to them through the prophets.

[11] Jung-Stilling describes this totalitarianism of Antichrist on the basis of Dan. 11:2; Thess. 2; and Apoc. 13: "Therefore, the man of sin will be a king, a great ruler whose power is untrammelled; for he will do whatever he wishes. He will forsake the religion of his fathers – the Christian religion – and will become its declared enemy; he will pass venomous and hostile enactments against the worship of God, forbid the Christian worship of God and initiate a vicious persecution of the true Christians. To do this without hindrance he will also draw to himself the highest spiritual power and join it to his earthly power. For he will establish himself in the temple of God and aim at total domination over all mankind, partly through his power, and partly by political means. He will shun women, and probably live in unnatural vice. Without any religion whatever, he will be a thoroughgoing humanist, atheist, and free thinker. He will exalt reason above everything, and his own reason will be his god, which all must worship and adore in him. Moreover, he will introduce a public cult, which will inevitably be warlike; for he will worship the god of war. He will be a professional warrior, because it is by force that he will maintain himself and will subject everything to himself. So he will value nothing but a good soldier, and he will reward them liberally. He alone will always be right; he will be a man who opposes both God and men." See *Erster Nachtrag zur Siegsgeschichte der christlichen Religion* (1805), pp. 95 et seq.

The meaning of προσκυνεῖν in the Apocalypse of St. John is examined by Joannes Horst in *Proskynein* (1932), pp. 253–91. This work also deals with the worship of the beast (pp. 263 et seq.), which "is a usurpation of the worship due to God alone in a horrible infernal travesty of the worship of God and the Lamb".

They cannot plead ignorance of its existence. They are not surprised about the beast and his malevolence towards them, for captivity and death are inseparable from war. But this is more than an earthly conflict. On the other hand, Christians will not rise against the beast; they are not political rebels. They do not worship it, but equally they do not fight it with the means of violence. They know that they form part of the still incomplete number of souls who are under the altar (6:9 et seq.), and that they will not escape suffering. Against the rage of the beast they show patience and faith; their patience draws life from the patience of Christ (cf. 3:10), and their faith is guaranteed by Christ.

According to the vision of the prophet, Antichrist is not only a political power, but also a spiritual force. He is a double being, and with the dragon he forms the "satanic trinity".[12] Part of the first beast is the "other beast" which rises from the earth (13:11), from the cosmos, and in the historical form which it then possessed, from Asia Minor, the homeland of prophets and cults in general, and of the emperor cult in particular.

This second beast complements the first beast; it adds two horns to the ten which the first beast already possesses, and perfects its power. It lacks the marks of power, and thereby it resembles a lamb. It frightens no one; it looks harmless and innocent, conceals its nature. As Primasius says, *Agnum fingit ut agnum invadat*. But when it opens its mouth and speaks, it speaks like a dragon. Speech seems to be its special task and vital element. This second beast could be described as the mouth of the dragon, its spokesman.

[12] Jung-Stilling, *Erklärung,* p. 392.

This chapter does not tell us as yet what this second beast is; but later (16:13, 19:20 and 20:10), we learn that it is "the false prophet", the collected strength of "the false prophets" (Mark 13:22), the effective spirit of false prophecy in concrete form. It is the agent of the first beast, instinct rather than spirit. In its service this second beast exercises the powers bestowed upon the first beast (13:12). It ensures that the first beast appears in public in the way it wishes. As a false prophet it is a religious, indeed priestly, power. We might remember that "the blending of the ritual institution with the administrative was a leading idea of the provincial organization of the imperial period".[13] Evidently the second beast is the priestly propagandist who invests the bestial power with a ritual, and thereby furthers its effectiveness.

That may also be inferred from the object which the second beast has set itself, and which it actually achieves, that the earth and its inhabitants should worship the ever-renewed political power (13:12). It is now clear how it is possible for men to be fascinated and bewildered when they are confronted with the beast. It is the work of a second power closely linked with the first. It is the spiritual power of Antichrist which causes the crafty, coarse and cruel empire to appear as the miracle worthy of adoration. In this way it ensures its political domination to be firm and imperishable. The spiritual instinct of the anti-Christian power leads men to believe in its perverted political reign.

The second beast employs three means to attain its end. Firstly, it performs wonderful signs (13:13). In both Christian

[13] Th. Mommsen, *The Provinces of the Roman Empire*, I, p. 345 (trans. W. P. Dickson, London 1886). See the general account which he gives there of conditions in Asia Minor.

and Jewish tradition it is held that the Antichrist performs signs and wonders.[14] The Messias, on the other hand, does not prove himself by miracles. The Antichrist has the power to perform miracles and signs, even the miraculous punishments, for which the disciples had asked Jesus and which he had refused them. But the Antichrist, while performing the miracle of Elias, is not on that account Elias. Such a miracle may lead men to believe, but in the beast and not in the Lamb. In both cases there is faith, but the faith is as different as the beast is from the Lamb. The miracles of false prophets mislead men in their faith. For they induce men to set up an image of the imperishable beast (13:14).

This is the second weapon of this political priesthood. For they also influence men through the image in which their submission to Satan, as well as faith in the beast, are expressed. This is not a lifeless image. It receives life from the skill and power of that imperial prophetic gift which allows men to see the depths of their god, "the depths of Satan" (2:24); it is capable of speech and action (13:15). Indeed, Satan has his image in that bestial perverted political power. And this power is presented to mankind through the word of its prophet. This chief priest entices men to make an image of the "eternal" beast, to realize its total terrestial power. This image is now to dominate men spiritually and physically. For the image of the new faith, the ritual image of Caesar and his might, will speak to men. It has intelligence, and produces intelligence; it appeals to the feelings, the reason and the will of its worshippers.

[14] In Selma Lagerlöf's novel *The Miracle of Antichrist,* he can perform even social miracles.

86

It not only intoxicates the masses, but also provides scholars with new and unforeseen tasks, it inspires the poets, and it arouses speculation. And the inscription on this image, which may be Αὐτοκράτορι θεῷ Δομιτιανῷ Καίσαρι Σεβαστῷ, is but the summing up of the spirit which through the image speaks words of admonition and consolation.

But the image also begins to act. Its intelligence, which penetrates public life, can bring it about that the refusal to worship the image of this god is punished with death. This intelligence is capable of deciding which men are to be counted loyal and god-fearing, and, therefore, deserving to live, and which are of the godless types who will not be tolerated in that religious empire. As the power of the beast is present in the image, the refusal to worship is equivalent to the total denial of this god. The crime of *laesae Romanae religionis* is simply *laesae maiestatis*. And how was a Christian to escape the death penalty, when his public refusal to worship Caesar and swear by his genius always raised the presumption that he had acted through *dolus,* the malice legally required for condemnation?[15] The image, supported and inspired by the prophetic force of political power, is thus an instrument by means of which the state can distinguish friends from enemies, and punish those who are enemies. The "intelligence" of the "image" ultimately constitutes a body of living law,[16] for the judges of this empire.[17]

[15] See R. Schütz, op. cit., pp. 30 et seq.

[16] In *Ludus de antichristo,* Antichrist sings: "I ascend to subject the world. I cast down the old. New laws are enacted."

[17] See also Erik Peterson in his essay "Der Geist der apostolischen Kirche nach der Geheimen Offenbarung" in *Hochland,* XXXIII, p. 67: "Ultimately power, being a mystery, calls for worship. The only problem

There is yet a third method by which the high priest of the anti-Christian power enforces the worship of its lord. The religion and the ritual which it prescribes are raised into the sphere of public life; a public profession is required of everyone (13:16–17). It is demanded that "all, both little and great, rich and poor, freemen and bondmen . . . have a character in their right hand or on their foreheads". Just as slaves and sacrificial animals were branded, so each man must show to whom he belongs, under whose protection and in whose service he is. The beast cannot entirely rely on his worshippers. It is dangerous when loyalty is confined to the heart and is expressed only by an occasional genuflection. The branded mark is the only way of identifying a slave. No man is, therefore, exempted from having this brand, an imitation of the invisible seal of Baptism recognizable only by faith. The beast needs above all the service of its great, rich, and free believers.

The mark is indelible. No one who has received it can rid himself of it. And a man's life depends on his mark: "That no man might buy or sell, but he that hath the character or the name of the beast, or the number of his name." Those who fail to profess the new religion publicly and unequivocally are cut off from society, are boycotted, and must perish from hunger.

The beast wants every single soul, and its resolute and mighty

is whether we will worship the lawful power of the Almighty, or the usurped power of him who makes himself like God. The Apocalypse tells us that the false prophet leads men to set up an image of Antichrist (13:14). What is a political symbol becomes an object of worship, and as such, it even works miracles (13:15). Division is created among men by the political symbol when it becomes an object of worship – the emperor worship in the Roman Empire is an example of this."

intelligence uses every means to ensure that none escapes him. He introduces a mark by which all those are recognized who are willing to sell themselves to him. Those who refuse the mark disturb his collective rule and are cut off.

Written on the mark is the name of the beast or the number of its name. This number of its name is intelligible, for it is not a demoniacal but a human name. The beast operates through a terrestial appearance. This appearance may be expressed in a variety of persons. But the appearance itself always remains the same. Its number is 666 (or 616). Its name is: καῖσαρ θεός.[18]

---

[18] There are many methods of explaining this number and as many different results. It is clear that today we have not the σοφία which the Apocalypse takes for granted. In the light of the context of chapter 13, and of the entire structure of the Apocalypse, I still consider that the solution adopted above is the most probable. It was suggested by Deissmann in *Licht vom Osten,* 4 th ed., p. 238, note 3.

Other QUAESTIONES DISPUTATAE:

KARL RAHNER, S.J.

Inspiration in the Bible

Karl Rahner, professor of dogmatic theology at Innsbruck, examines the question of scriptural inspiration with the conviction that the whole issue could benefit by being completely re-thought. He suggests, therefore, an entirely new approach to the mystery, in which the Scriptures are seen primarily as an essential and constitutive element of the Apostolic Church, and their inspiration simply as part of the activity of God in establishing the Church as the guardian of the deposit of faith. The study is intentionally provocative, but no one conversant with the subject of inspiration can fail to find here food for thought and reflection.

KARL RAHNER, S.J.

On the Theology of Death

The author treats of the nature of the Christian's death from the theological point of view and on the special mode of death called martyrdom. He is concerned with opening up new perspectives in older problems, striving to formulate new and more fruitful concepts for the penetration of one of the most important dimensions of Christian belief and experience. Writing with the great care necessary in theological discussion and abstaining from technical terminology and "jargon", he conveys a sense of the intellectual urgency and the exploratory nature of the enquiry. This book forms part of a new series of short treatises entitled *Quaestiones Disputatae*, in which some of the more urgent, "open" questions of the Christian faith are discussed by eminent Catholic writers.